D1349635

# From Edison to iPod

## PROTECT YOUR IDEAS AND MAKE MONEY

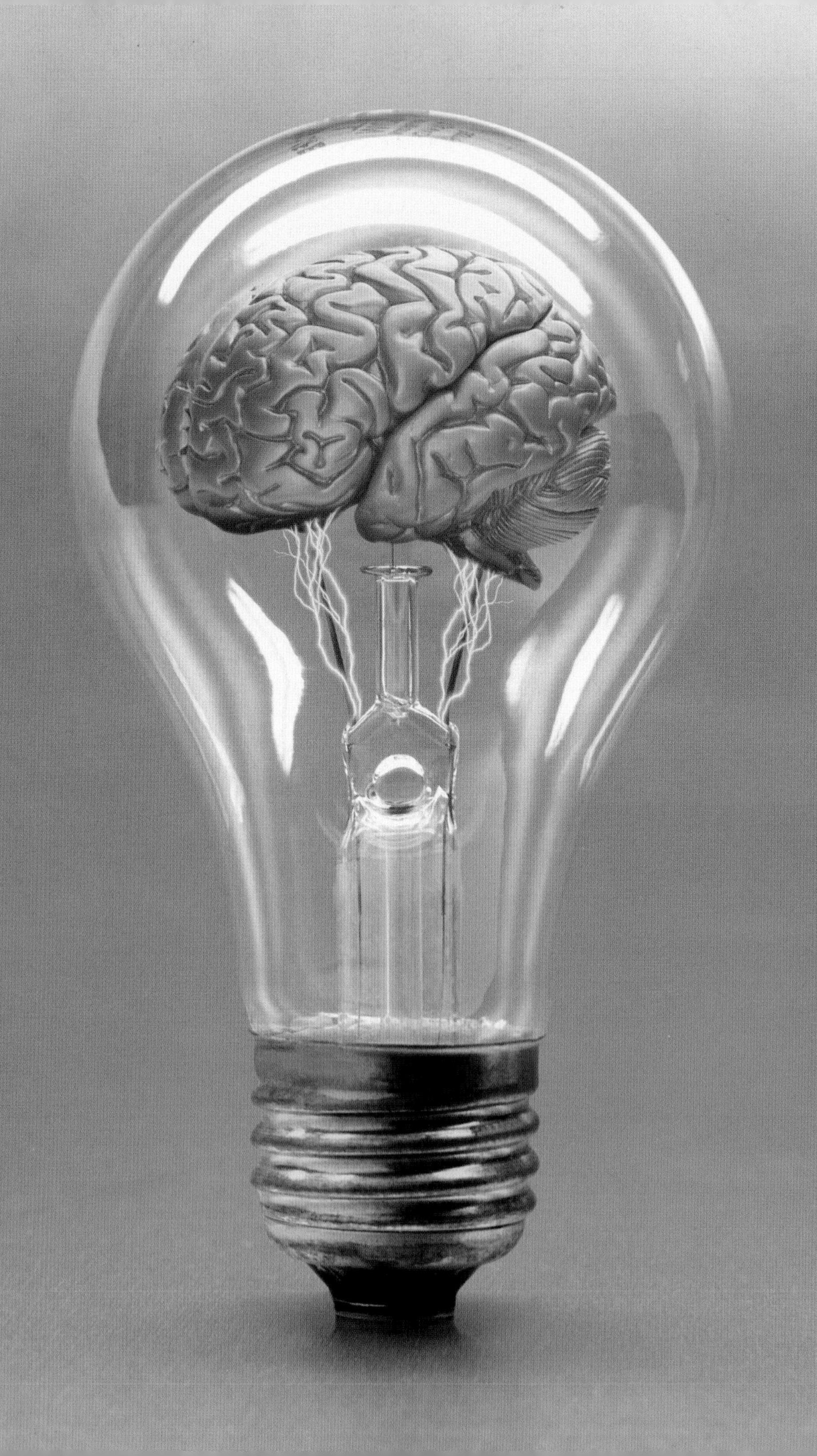

FREDERICK MOSTERT

# From Edison to iPod

## PROTECT YOUR IDEAS AND MAKE MONEY

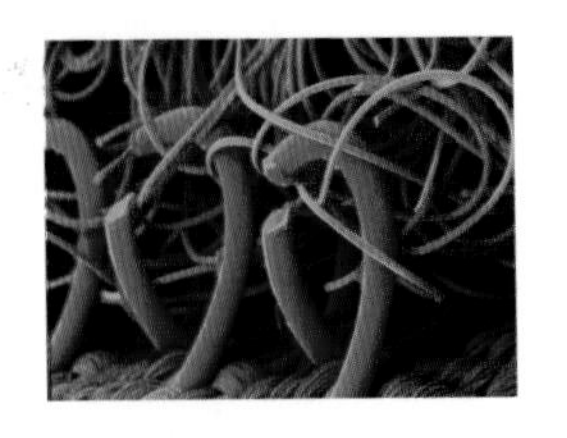

DK

LONDON, NEW YORK, MUNICH, MELBOURNE, DELHI

IN MEMORY OF THAT REMARKABLE JUDGE, MY FATHER

**Editor** Elizabeth Watson
**Senior Art Editor** Helen Spencer
**Executive Managing Editor** Adèle Hayward
**Managing Art Editor** Nick Harris
**DTP Designer** Traci Salter
**Production Controller** Luca Frassinetti
**Art Director** Peter Luff
**Publishing Director** Corinne Roberts

**Designed for DK by** Bill Mason

First published in Great Britain in 2007 by
Dorling Kindersley Limited,
80 Strand, London WC2R 0RL
A Penguin Company

2 4 6 8 10 9 7 5 3 1



A CIP catalogue record for this book is available from the British Library.

ISBN: 978-1-4053-1926-3



Reproduced by MDP in the UK
Printed and bound by Leo Paper Products Ltd in China
Discover more at www.dk.com

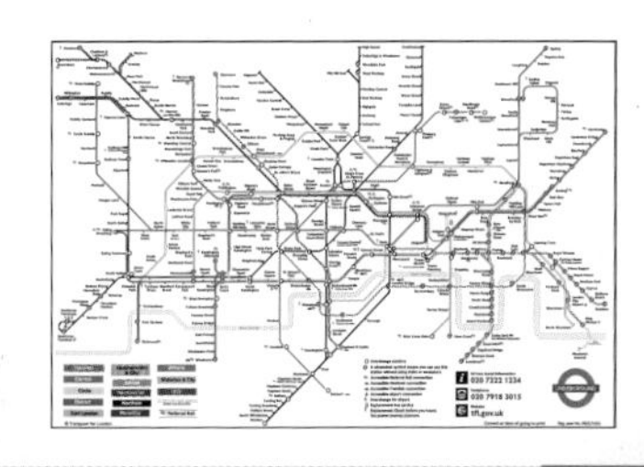



## DISCLAIMER

All information in this book is provided to the public as a source of general information on intellectual property issues. In legal matters, no publication – whether in printed or electronic form – can take the place of professional advice given with full knowledge of the specific facts and laws that apply. While reasonable effort has been made to ensure the accuracy of the information in this book, it should not be treated as the basis for formulating business decisions without professional advice. It should be emphasized that intellectual property laws vary from country to country, and between jurisdictions within some countries. Throughout the book I have indicated some particular instances where legal advice should be sought. This is indicated by the "see your lawyer" icon demonstrated below. The examples and references to intellectual property in this book do not constitute any judgement or view by the publisher or authors as to the validity or enforceability, or lack thereof, and are intended solely for educational purposes only.

## KEY TO SYMBOLS

! Note of caution: something to be aware of

Definition: a jargon-busting explanation of legal terms

Debunking the myth: sets straight common misbeliefs

Legal test: factors the law takes into account when addressing an issue

Good news!

While you should always work with a lawyer, this is a special reminder

Useful resources

? Indicates a whole-page feature addressing a particular concern

Indicates a list of examples

# contents



You can also find more information at www.fromedisontoipod.com

# introduction



Intellectual property has become a household issue. From the boardroom to internet chat rooms, and even in gossip columns, intellectual property is a hot topic. But what exactly is it? How does it affect you? If you make it big, isn't this something your lawyers can just take care of? Or you might modestly conclude that you are not an intellectual, you do not have any property, and therefore there is no way that understanding intellectual property would matter to you.

It matters! Understanding intellectual property can help you protect an incredible creation and parlay it into a valuable asset that you can exploit, license, or sell. Without a grasp of intellectual property, you may unwittingly give your creation away. Adopting a few safeguards can make the difference between building a business and regretting missed opportunities. And when intellectual property is approached as a whole, it becomes a reliable tool available to you and your business: a resource that you can put to work.

If you are a creative person, like a designer, an artist or a musician, an entrepreneur with unique concepts, or a marketer, or if you are an investor who is frequently approached with new ideas, this is a good guidebook.

The internet and other technological advances have given our generation immediate access to endless information. Corporate downsizing has introduced more individual entrepreneurs and consultants to the marketplace and the global economy makes it essential to have knowledge and tools available to remain competitive. Cultural and business climates have evolved to a point where many people are sophisticated enough to know their creation is entitled to valuable intellectual property rights. But you may be unsure as to how to protect these rights. What's the difference between a patent and a design right? A trade mark and a copyright? What's a trade secret, and how does it differ from a trade name? What about domain names? These categories might sound like far-off places and all you have is a blurry out-of-date road map to find your way. But when all these areas of intellectual property are understood and approached holistically, you will have the power to make good business decisions and get the most out of your creations.

Since the 1980s, I have watched an interest in and awareness of intellectual property skyrocket. At social and family gatherings, I have gone from watching eyes glaze over as I explain what I do to being asked very specific questions about a particular issue someone is facing. These days I attend social gatherings armed with pen and notepad because I am almost always cornered by someone looking for some "quick" advice on how to protect a new creation. For example, how to protect a recipe for a new pastry creation, a new website design, an idea for an innovative bracelet, or a restaurant name. I have advised a wide variety of individuals, including watch and jewellery designers, chefs, physical fitness trainers, opera singers, restaurateurs, computer scientists, fashion designers, doctors, fragrance houses, architects, corporate finance specialists, symphony orchestras, and many other entrepreneurs. My work has included looking after the interests of not-for-profit organizations and charities as well as working with and advising celebrities and public figures, including Nelson Mandela, Michael Douglas, Catherine Zeta-Jones, Jackie Chan, Sylvester Stallone, Ernie Els, Boris Becker, Stella McCartney, and the Shaolin Monks. However divergent their interests, all these people share one common characteristic – a creative spirit. Not only have they made use of their imaginations, they also possess enthusiasm, optimism, and pride in their creations. They come to me to help them get the right kind of protection.

10

For me, the joy of intellectual property is the fact that I deal with the creative initiatives of people who come up with excellent ideas. Indeed, I am exposed to the cutting edge of intellectual creation, which can often be converted to useful commercial gain.

Given these needs, I have written this practical guide to demystify intellectual property. My goal is to reveal the secrets and explain the complexities and formalities of the law, steering clear of legal jargon. I have mapped out the array of intellectual property options available to you and explained how you can develop strategies and practices to protect your creations. I have also included hands-on tips and deeper insights based on many years of advising clients in this field. I like to fancy myself as a tour guide taking you on a trip through the world of intellectual property. While the different categories – trade marks, copyright, trade secrets, etc. – are destinations in themselves, as any good traveller knows, you need to take in the local colour to really understand a place. It would be a shame to walk away from this book thinking that intellectual property is a bunch of disjointed, unrelated fields. Don't treat it like, "If it's Tuesday, I must be in patents." And, like any good trip, a second visit will bring better understanding. First, read this book in its entirety to see how you can start to apply it in your day-to-day business. Then re-read the sections that are most relevant right now. Finally, re-read the other sections to see whether they may apply later on. But remember, each case depends on its individual facts. Intellectual property laws are filled with nuances and exceptions to the rule. While you may want to try some of this on your own, I can't stress enough how important it is to have a trusted intellectual property lawyer who can advise and guide you through the varying terrain.

When know-how and creativity come together and you manage to create something of intellectual value, it is a great achievement. Well done. Now let's get down to the business of making sure the rights to your brainchild are protected.

# the basics



## THE GOLDEN RULES

There are two golden rules that will assist you greatly in understanding the fundamentals of intellectual property rights.

### Rule number one: first in time, first in right

The one who is first past the post – whether it is tortoise or hare – wins. This holds true in fairy tales and in real life. In the past, for example, water laws operated on the same basis: the individual who first actively diverted water from a stream for beneficial use had the first right to use the water. Many intellectual property cases turn on proving who was the first to establish a specific intellectual property.

If you are the first person to file a patent application on a new invention, such as a uniquely engineered safe-seal bottle top or a design right application on a uniquely designed lamp, or if you are first to use a trade mark such as a cool name or hip logo for your product or service, or first to write down words for a new song which have been going through your head, or you have designed a new website in source code, you are in a far better position to protect the intellectual property in your creation and to win any legal battles along the way.

In this guide I will show you how best to employ practical tips to your advantage. They should enable you to demonstrate convincingly that you were the first to establish a particular intellectual property right.

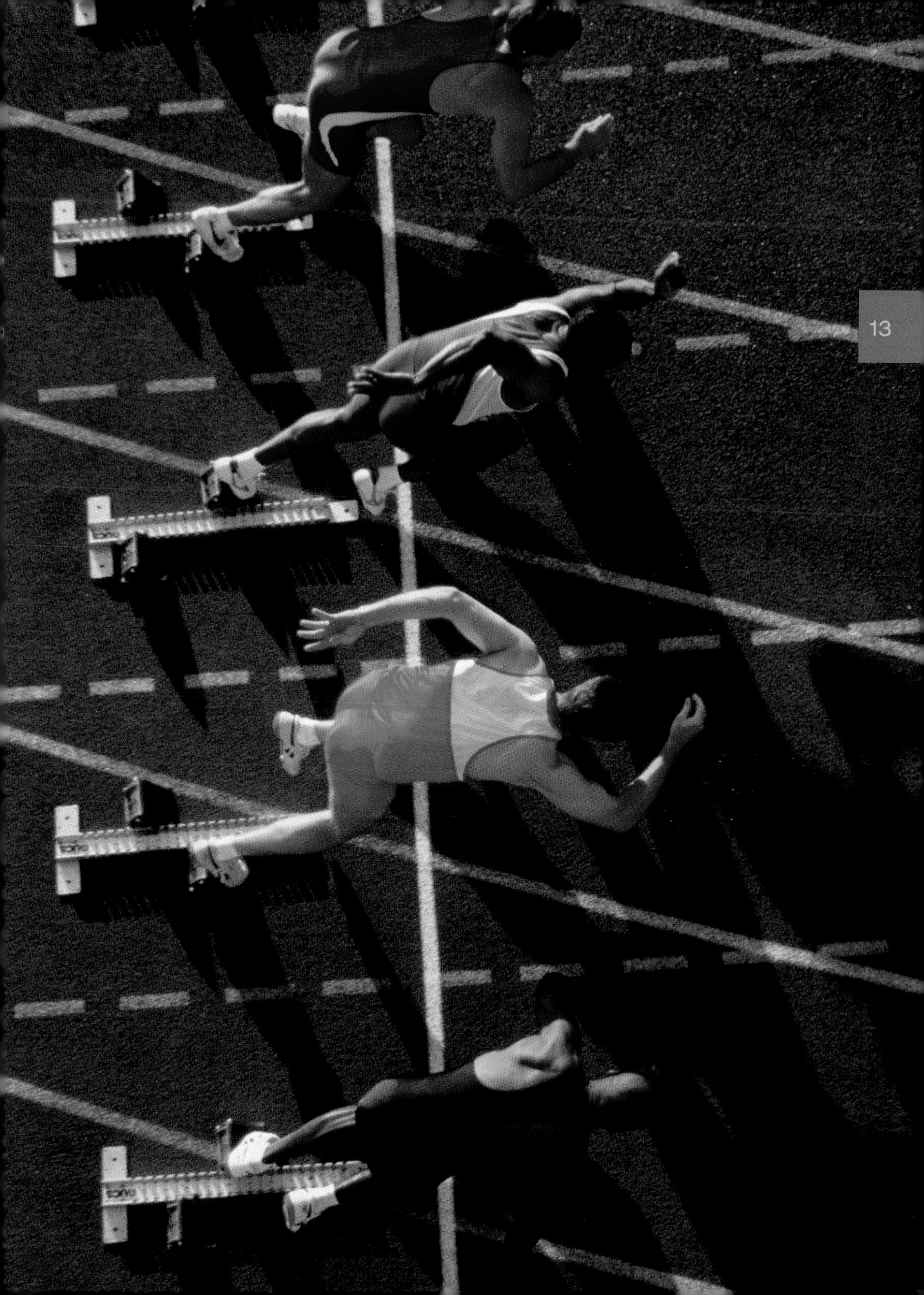

### Rule number two: ideas alone are not protectable

We all have ideas and dreams. But that doesn't put money in the bank. When you come up with a specific idea, lay it out and do something with it. The result might be a painting, a play, an improved way to use debit cards on the internet, a new name for your jewellery line, or a great design for a mobile phone. All of these are "creations", which can be protected by different and overlapping categories of intellectual property. But only if you get your idea out of your head and into action.

## WHY BOTHER PROTECTING INTELLECTUAL PROPERTY?

This book is not intended to be a history lesson to explain how and why intellectual property came about or how it is evolving. These are very interesting topics and, in fact, at some point you may want to read more about them. But my purpose here is to get you to focus on how you can protect your creations. To do that I will spend a moment to explain that, in the UK and many other countries, the driving force behind intellectual property is that society wants to reward and provide incentives to creative

individuals who come up with new creations. This isn't because our society is a great humanitarian culture, although it may be. The reason here is economic. Using candles and kerosene at night-time might sound quaint, but it is a big hassle. It starts fires. And it is not very effective, unless your goal is romance. So people like Thomas Edison came along and we know how that story goes. Society wants to encourage more than patentable inventions. It provides copyright protection to the authors and visual artists of our time who can collect royalties for their works. The same is true in the commercial world with design rights. Design rights are available to protect the fruits of market studies and product research. They enable the owners to carve out special niches so that designs can be exploited exclusively. Trade marks are similarly protected on the basis of perceived societal benefit. Consumers need to be safeguarded against deception and confusion by counterfeiters and infringers who falsely trade on the name and reputation of the original owners. It is in this tradition of providing incentives to create that most of the intellectual property laws have been written. You can be assured that both government and our society encourage you to be innovative and reward those who are first to create and protect something of value. Most intellectual property rights are protected on the premise that society as a whole benefits from new scientific inventions and artistic works of creative individuals. Creative spirits, like you, should be incentivized to continue to produce works for the betterment of the community. The best way to accomplish this goal is to grant such creative individuals exclusive rights to their creations for limited periods of time. Your creations, whatever they are, need and deserve protection. Although free competition in the marketplace is encouraged, it should be fair. Consequently, the law is designed to protect you from unconscionable competitors who steal your intellectual property. For example, the brand name of your product can be protected by a registered trade mark, your new invention of a computer-coded wizard to authenticate online sales can be safeguarded by a patent registration, your secret recipe and formula for a pastry creation can be shielded by trade secret law, your distinctive design for a new perfume bottle can be covered by a design right, and your original design for a unique website or sculpture can be protected by copyright.





## The other side of the coin

That you are entitled to benefit from your creative intellectual endeavours and that such rights should be yours in perpetuity seems only fair and stems from a basic sense of natural justice. But little in life is black and white. Just as society rewards you, it also needs to draw lines and limit the boundaries of intellectual property rights. Free speech, including the right to know, needs to be considered when the media broadcast news items. And handing over inventions to the public for use and development without charge comes at the end of a patent.

# Trade marks can't be like unused toys on the playground. Either you use them or they are there for someone else to use.



In a free and idea-rich society such as ours, creative spirits need to be nurtured and encouraged so that the creative process can prosper. No man is an island and we rely on each other for insight and inspiration. Creative spirits must be able to draw on prior inventions and artistic works in order to reach even greater heights. Even a genius such as Sir Isaac Newton admitted with humility, "If I have seen further it is by standing on the shoulders of giants".

A creative spirit thrives on past experiences, prior inventions, and previously experienced artistic works. This is the way our civilization has advanced for years and nothing I have seen in over two decades of experience has caused me to believe that it is changing. In fact, the more that new ideas emerge into creations, the more exciting and endless it seems. I have watched the internet unfold and develop from a simple communications jalopy to an entire platform and medium for living and doing business. What will be next? Perhaps one of you reading this book knows. In fact, I bet that a number of you might have the next big ideas. I want to help you navigate your way through the world of intellectual property so that, as your ideas evolve into creations, you will know which types of intellectual property rights you have and how they can be protected.

# trade marks



## DEFINITION

Trade marks are the words, designs, and other markings that identify and distinguish products or services from one another. They are the link between the maker and the customer, and they help consumers distinguish between competing brands. Trade marks can suggest a certain quality or status (think **CARTIER** versus **SWATCH**) and they serve the public interest by protecting consumers from being deceived or misled by substandard products.

## DURATION

Indefinite, as long as the trade mark is used. As protection flows from use, you need to use them or you lose them. Trade marks often become your most valuable intellectual property after other assets have expired.

◀ **Logo marks**
The iconic Apple logo symbolizes the harmony of excellence in design and computer science. This Apple logo must be one of the most recognized logos throughout the world. The clean design of the logo itself underscores the virtue of simplicity in design.

Trade marks are words, designs, and other markings that identify and distinguish products or services from one another.





Kodak

**Word marks**

The word Kodak was first registered as a trade mark in 1888 and was "invented" by George Eastman, "I devised the name myself. The letter 'K' had been a favourite with me – it seems a strong, incisive sort of letter. It became a question of trying out a great number of combinations of letters that made words starting and ending with 'K'. The word 'Kodak' is the result."

**Logo marks**

This logo was given to the monks of the Shaolin Temple by a prince of the Ming Dynasty around 1500 AD. It symbolizes the Temple's harmonic fusion of Taoism, Confucianism, and Buddhism. The Shaolin Temple has since stylized this ancient symbol to reflect the Temple's heritage and history. The first character, looking directly at you, represents Buddhism, while the two characters who look at each other, on the left and right of the circle, represent Confucianism and Taoism. This logo can be used only by those who have a direct connection to the Temple – an interesting case of trade mark law protecting cultural values and heritage.

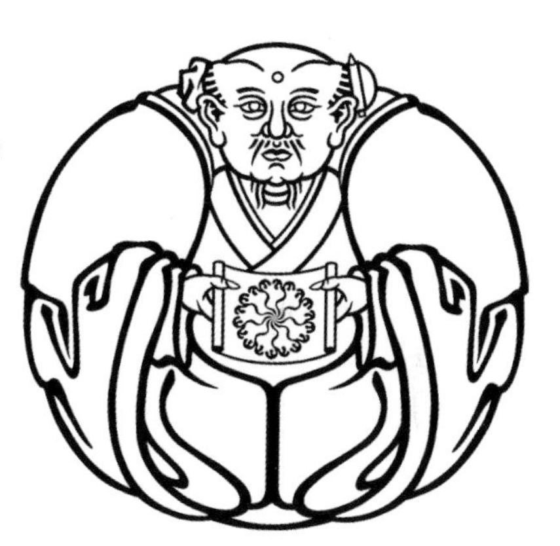

**Logo marks**

The subject of a trade mark may bear no logical relation to the particular product on which it is used, but can become closely associated with that specific product over time. This Penguin logo has become so internationally synonymous with books that, while in solitary confinement in Beirut, hostage Terry Waite drew a picture of a penguin to communicate to his guard his request for some good reading material. And he was understood!

As protection for trade marks flows from use, you have to use them or you lose them.





## HOW TO PROTECT IT

- Through extensive use on your product or service.
- Seriously consider registration with the Trade Marks Office.

## TIPS

- Select a strong mark.
- Keep records of use of the mark, especially the date of first use.
- Obtain a trade mark search before use or filing to avoid disappointment and evaluate risk.
- Consider adopting the same domain name or trade name as your trade mark.
- Police and enforce your trade mark.
- Use ® for registered and ™ for unregistered trade marks as a warning on your product or service.

▲ **Logo marks**
"Shell" was first used as a trade mark by Marcus Samuel and Company in 1891 for paraffin shipped from London to East Asia. This small business originally sold antiques, curios, and, most notably, oriental seashells. The first logo, a mussel shell, was introduced in 1901 and morphed into a scallop shell or "pecten" logo in 1904 and has remained the symbol of the Royal Dutch-Shell Group ever since.

## EXAMPLES

**HEINZ**, **IPOD**, **LINUX**, **MERCEDES-BENZ** star symbol, the **COCA-COLA** contour bottle, the shape of the **MORGAN** car, **DHL**, the name **ROBBIE WILLIAMS**, **DAVID BECKHAM**'s signature, the colour of **VEUVE CLICQUOT** labels, the **ADIDAS** three stripes design.

**◄ Combination marks**
Heinz is a classic trade mark, consisting of an internationally known name, "Heinz", and a logo. Heinz is famous for its "57 Varieties" slogan in the US and the advertising jingle "Beanz Meanz Heinz" in the UK. It was founded in 1869 in Sharpsburg, Pennsylvania, by Henry John Heinz and its first products were processed condiments delivered to local greengrocers by horse-drawn carriages. In 1876, the company launched tomato ketchup. And the rest is history.



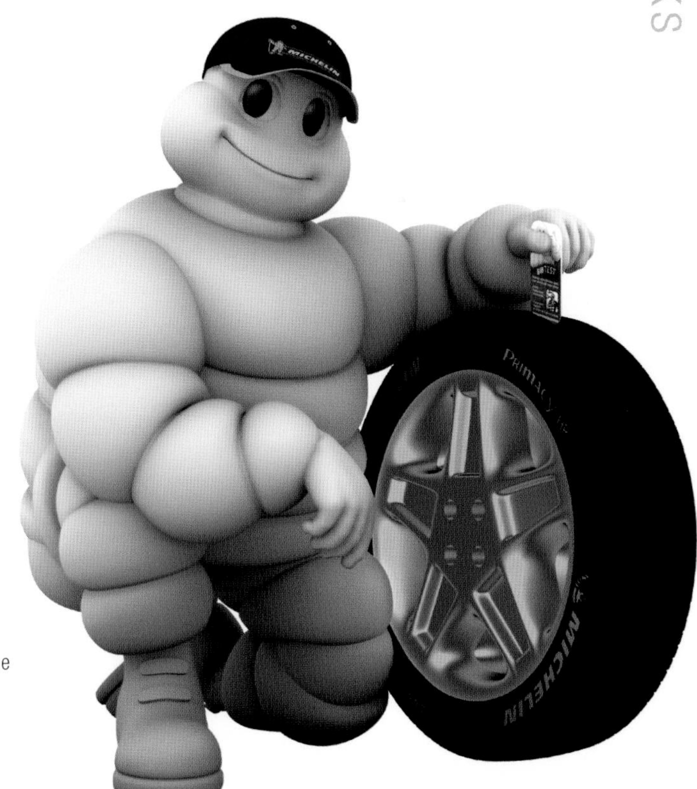


**► The Michelin Man**
Bibendum, or the Michelin Man, has been the key symbol of the French tyre company since 1898. It is said that Mr O'Galop, the creator of this logo, derived his inspiration from a stack of rubber tyres. A highly active *bon vivant*, Bibendum's feel-good energy is used as a marketing tool. The famous art nouveau Michelin building in Chelsea, London, houses a well-known restaurant under the name of Bibendum, which pays homage to the character Bibendum to this day.

# copyright



## DEFINITION

Copyright covers works of art in the broadest sense. The moment you use your own ingenuity to create an original story, poem, article, or even software, you automatically have copyright in your creation. However, in order to qualify, a work must have been rendered in a tangible medium: only the physical expression of an idea is protected, not the idea itself. As well as an economic right, some copyright owners also have moral rights. These protect the way in which your work is used and is attributed to you.

## DURATION

For the life of the creator plus 70 years for most works.

Registered User No. 06/E/1655

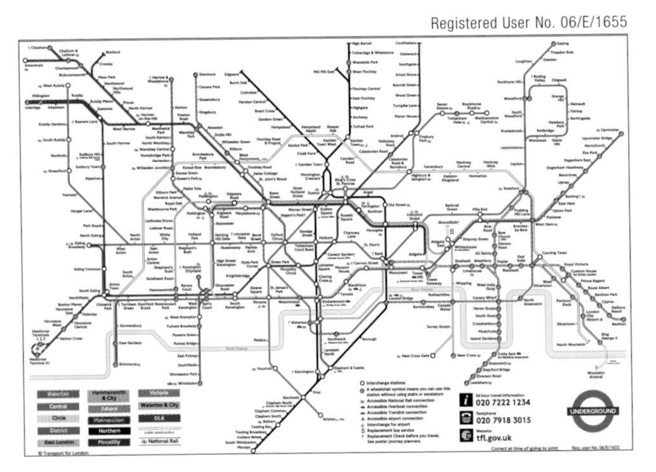

◄ **Maps**

In 1933, Harry Beck, an Underground electrical draughtsman, persuaded London Transport to abandon its traditional, free-flowing map and use a diagrammatic map in its place. Beck's training as an electrical engineer led to a vertical and horizontal map with 45-degree angles that is supremely user-friendly. The essential tool for all users of the London Underground, it has become a template for transport maps throughout the world.

The moment you use your own ingenuity to create an original story, poem, article, or even software, you have copyright in your creation.

▲ **Sculptures**

*The Kiss* by Auguste Rodin (1901–1904) has become ubiquitous worldwide as a symbol of love. This masterpiece depicts the lovers Paulo Malatesta and Francesca da Rimini, who were slain by Francesca's incensed husband and immortalized in Dante's *Inferno*.

▲ **Musical scores**

*The Entertainer*, written in 1902 by ragtime musician Scott Joplin, has become synonymous with snooker on BBC television. Snooker champion Steve Davis listens to the quirky piano rag before matches to get him in the mood. It has also found new life as a novelty ringtone in the UK.

► **Paintings**

The *Mona Lisa* (1503–1506), with her enigmatic smile, is often named as the most instantly recognizable piece of art in the world. Leonardo da Vinci's famous lady has her home in the Louvre in Paris. Da Vinci was so fond of this painting that he is said to have carried it with him wherever he went.

### HOW TO PROTECT IT

- It is automatic on the date of creation.
- As registration is not available in the UK, you could consider obtaining a registration through the US Copyright Office.

### TIPS

- Date and sign or stamp to show proof of ownership.
- Consider obtaining notary or third-party confirmation of date of creation or a statutory declaration.
- Use a copyright legend as a warning: © 2007. John Smith. All rights reserved.

▲ **Tattoos**
Even tattoos can attract copyright if the design is original and unique. However, the person who has the design tattooed on his or her body may not be the owner of the copyright. That right belongs to the original tattoo artist.

### EXAMPLES

Literature, writings, computer software and source code, visual designs, logos, photographs, jewellery designs, architectural drawings, the design of a web page, radio and television broadcasts, motion pictures (including DVDs), sound recordings (including CDs and downloads), dress designs, play scripts, sculptures, articles written for magazines, journals, etc., and engineering drawings.

As a copyright holder, you also have moral rights. These protect the way in which your work is used and attributed to you.



▶ **Intricate jewellery designs**
The jewellery piece shown here depicts an elegant snake and is an example of the type of unique and elaborate jewellery designs that can be protected by copyright. Copyright protection on such three-dimensional designs is an effective way of building up your arsenal of intellectual property rights so you can protect against cheap knock-offs.

## RIGHTS OF PUBLICITY

In the United States, another right that can be protected is known as the "right of publicity". This protects the name, likeness, voice, and other characteristics of celebrities and people who have "selling power". This right can last for as long as 100 years after death. Even though these rights exist and can be very useful in the United States, if you plan to use or license your name as a logo with your image or some other trait you have for specific products and services, it is also a good idea to file a trade mark application and get the necessary domain name registrations before you become too popular. Outside the United States, where this "right of publicity" is not recognized, obtaining trade mark registrations and domain name registrations is your best option.

# design rights



### DEFINITION

Design rights protect the two-dimensional and three-dimensional appearance or ornamental shape of an item. To qualify, an object must have a specific appearance that can be visually recognized: a design right has nothing to do with the task an item performs.

### DURATION

Unregistered designs: 10 years after the first marketing of the product, but no longer than 15 years from the date of creation. Registered designs: 25 years from the date of filing.

▲ **Package designs**
Like any type of packaging, blister packs for pills or other items can be worthy of design protection. With so much potential variation, it is no surprise that dozens of designs have been registered for packaging worldwide.

Design rights protect the two- or three-dimensional appearance or ornamental shape of a product or its packaging.

▶ **Designer handbags**

One of the key distinguishing features of the iconic Silverado Chloe bag is the embroidery inspired by a vintage bag bought in a flea market, providing a feminine touch and giving the bag its "Chloe Spirit". The design process for this bag was unusual in that it took only one month from first drawing through to final prototype.

▼ **Motorcar designs**

The E-type Jaguar (1961) is considered one of the sexiest sports cars ever launched and the crowning glory of Sir William Lyons, founder of the Jaguar motor company. A take on its racing sibling, the D-type Jaguar, the E-type won the Le Mans 24-hour endurance race five times.

The shape was the brainchild of ex-aircraft-industry specialist Malcolm Sayer, who combined artistic flair with wind-flow dynamics when designing the car's contours. The E-type Jaguar is often the only car on display at the Museum of Modern Art in New York.

Consider a search before filing to avoid disappointment or huge expenses.





### HOW TO PROTECT IT

- Unregistered design rights: are automatic on the date of creation.
- Registered design rights: consider registering your design to help show proof of ownership.

### TIPS

- Date and sign or stamp your work to show proof of ownership.
- Consider obtaining notary or third-party confirmation of the date of creation, or a statutory declaration.
- Consider a search before filing to avoid disappointment or huge expenses.
- Don't disclose your invention before filing!

### EXAMPLES

The design of a perfume bottle, an ornamental necklace, the shape of a new car, distinctive packaging for a product, the shape of a biscuit, the shape of a new handbag.

◄ **Computer hardware**
A design icon when it was launched in 1998, the iMac doubled Apple's profits within five months of its launch and has become one of the most distinctive computer designs of all time.

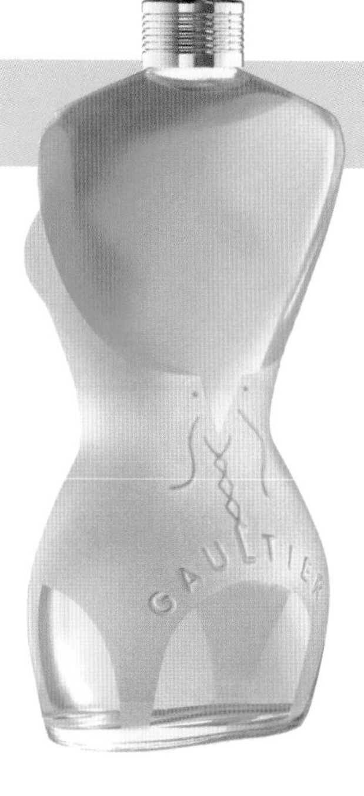


▲ **Perfume bottles**
This unique, distinctive perfume bottle design by Jean-Paul Gaultier has become a classic example of design in the perfume world. In designing this icon, Jean-Paul Gaultier was inspired by Madonna wearing her trade mark bustier. The design is completed by a powdered glass dusting.

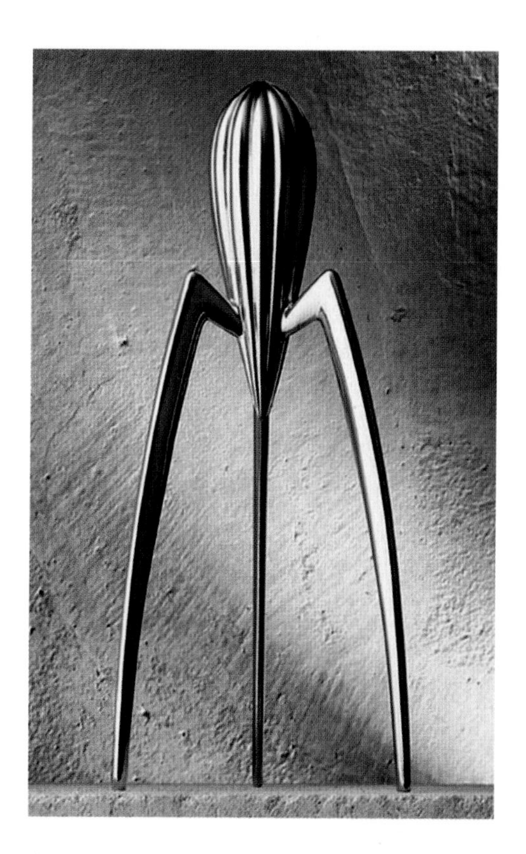

▲ **Product designs**
This lemon squeezer was designed by Philippe Starck in 1990. Bizarrely, the product is now more famous as a design icon than as a useful kitchen implement. This product proves the point that everyday objects can become true design icons.

# trade secrets



## DEFINITION

Trade secrets refer to confidential business information, such as formulas, technical know-how, computer code, recipes, and customer and supply lists. This information is very valuable to organizations and takes time and effort to develop. Keeping it confidential is critical to your business; otherwise your product or service could lose its competitive edge. Information is not a trade secret if it can be reverse engineered. Reverse engineering is where the competition can, through careful analysis, figure out the unique components, their composition, and relative quantity.

## DURATION

For as long as the trade secret remains confidential and is not disclosed or reverse engineered.

◀ **Computer code**
Instead of patents, various aspects of software, including its source code, may be protected by trade secrets. It is generally hard to reverse engineer object code (the sequence of 1s and 0s that execute instructions) in order to obtain a source code. Patents protecting software often disclose algorithms, but this is not the case for trade secrets. Hence, many developers prefer the trade secret route.

Trade secrets refer to confidential business information. This information is very valuable to organizations.

▲ **Secret formulas**

The Coca-Cola formula, Merchandise 7X, is probably one of the most talked-about trade secrets in the world. This secret formula was developed by John Pemberton, a pharmacist from Georgia, in 1886. The Coca-Cola Company has always remained tight-lipped regarding this formula and it is believed that only a few executives have full knowledge of the secret at any time.

## Information is not classified as a trade secret if it can be reverse engineered.





▶ **Secret recipes**

Famous recipes such as those for chocolate truffles can be protected by trade secrets. Chef Bill McCarrick, master chocolatier of Sir Hans Sloane Chocolate & Champagne House, says, "My most important new chocolate creations are kept carefully confidential and are protected as trade secrets".

### HOW TO PROTECT IT

- Keep it secret.
- Have good practices in place to prove you maintain a secure workplace.

### TIPS

- Have business partners, subcontractors, and employees sign a confidentiality letter or nondisclosure agreement to show proof of confidentiality.

### EXAMPLES

Formulas, the combination of fragrances in a perfume, the ingredients in some chocolate truffles, the know-how that helps you to manufacture a product and get it to market effectively, a proposal for a television series, customer lists belonging to a business, a method of manufacture, marketing plans, survey methods used by professional pollsters.

▲ **Secret recipes**
Colonel Harland Sanders developed the secret KFC formula, which includes 11 herbs and spices, when he operated the Sanders Court & Café from a roadside restaurant in Corbin, Kentucky, in the 1930s. Although this trade secret is now locked up in a vault in Louisville, Kentucky, Colonel Sanders used to carry the secret formula in his head and kept the spice mixture in his car. Very few people today know the billion-dollar recipe and they have all signed nondisclosure agreements.

► **Secret recipes**
This recipe is a unique trade secret. John Lea and William Perrins, owners of a pharmacy, prepared a sauce according to instructions given to them by a certain Lord Sandys, who had brought the recipe back from Bengal. The sauce, however, was disappointing, so was left and forgotten in their cellars. Rediscovered after a few years, the sauce was tasted again. Much to the amazement of the pharmacists, the matured sauce had turned into a taste sensation. They capitalized on their find, which became a worldwide success. The recipe has been secret for over 160 years and at any moment only three or four people know what special ingredient gives Lea & Perrins its extra oomph!

Patents can cover any invention, but most are in the fields of science and technology.



# patents



## DEFINITION

Patents can cover any invention, but most are in the fields of science and technology. They protect a basic product and the way it is made, as well as specific features for that product or process. New patents can cover existing inventions that have been expanded or built on to make them better, easier, cheaper, or more efficient to use. Patents cover hundreds of thousands of products and processes all around you, ranging from vitamin pills to flat-screen televisions, from the windscreen wiper on your car to a pacemaker.

## DURATION

Twenty years from the date of filing the patent application at the Patent Office.

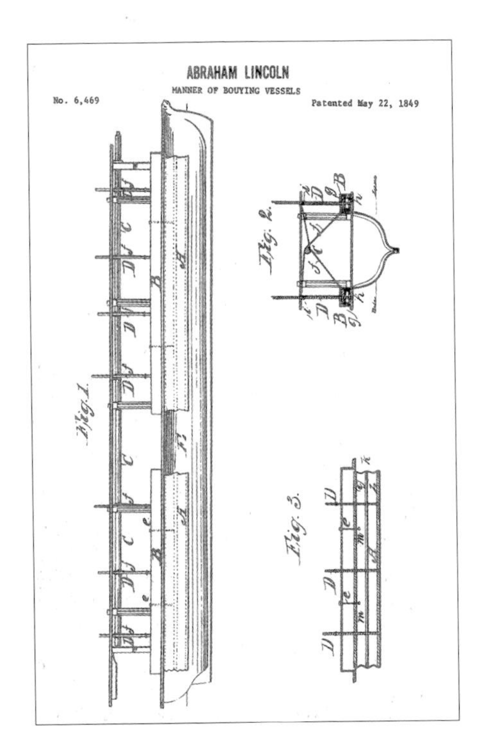


◀ **Abraham Lincoln**
The only US president to have held a patent (US Patent No. 6,469), Abraham Lincoln was granted his patent on 22 May 1849 for an invention to lift boats over shoals. A scale model is on display at the Smithsonian Institution in Washington, DC.

**Jamie Lee Curtis**

Jamie Lee Curtis is the proud owner of US Patent No. 4,753,647, which was granted in 1988 for a nappy with a moisture-proof pocket capable of holding one or more clean-up wipes. Stylish and useful.

**Edison light bulb**

The light bulb is one of Thomas Edison's most famous inventions. A prolific filer of patents, Edison had close to 1,100 patents to his name.

**VELCRO® fabric**

Inspiration for patent inventions can occur when walking your dogs. George de Mestral's dogs would be covered in burr seeds when he took them walking along the foothills of the Swiss Alps. By examining the burr seeds more closely, Mestral noticed that they projected hook-like teeth, which enabled them to stick firmly to the coats of his pets. He was thus inspired to invent a two-pronged fastener. He coined the word **VELCRO** as a trade mark from the words "velour" and "crochet". The patent was granted in Switzerland in 1954.

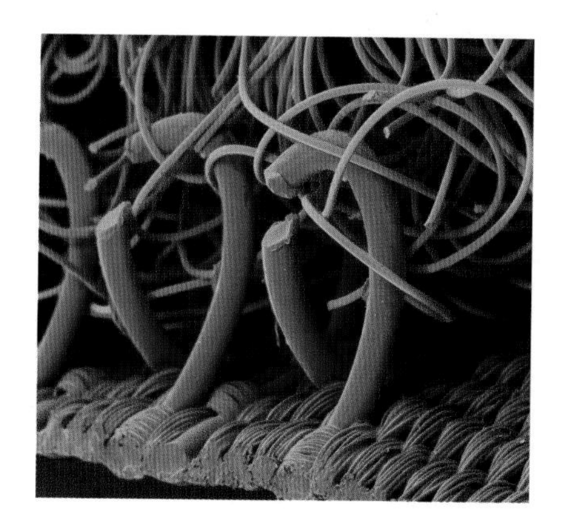

### HOW TO PROTECT IT

- Through registration at the Patent Office.
- Don't disclose your invention before filing!

### TIPS

- Run to the Patent Office to beat the competition.
- Before filing, keep good records and date them.
- Consider a patent search before filing to avoid disappointment or huge expenses.
- Have business partners, subcontractors, and employees sign confidentiality letters or nondisclosure agreements until you are on file.

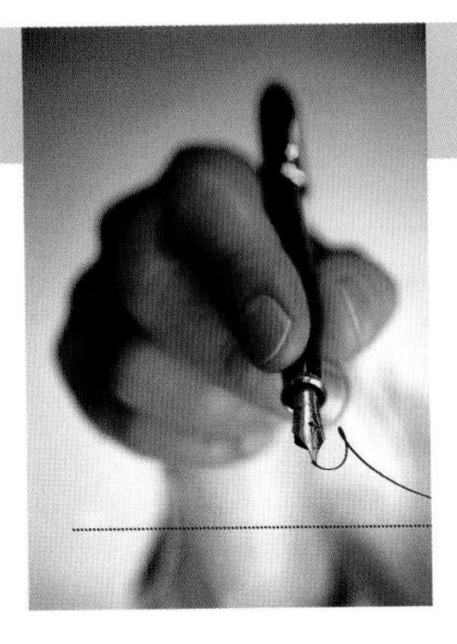

▲ **Fountain pens**
Everyday objects such as pens often embody patented inventions. Famous names like Parker, Sheaffer, and Waterman dot the patent landscape of the late 19th and early 20th centuries with their fountain pen innovations. Laszlo Biro later patented the modern ballpoint pen, now often simply referred to as a "Biro", before then selling his rights to Bic.

### EXAMPLES

The telephone, the light bulb, online retail procedures, pharmaceuticals, certain computer programs, ballpoint pens, vacuum cleaners, windsurf boards and rigging, the computer mouse, the cut of a diamond, artificial heart valves, methods for downloading music, plastics. ADOBE's ACROBAT READER program is covered by no fewer than 40 patents and the company ALTA VISTA owns more than 50 search engine patents.

They protect a basic product and the way it is made, as well as specific features for that product or process.





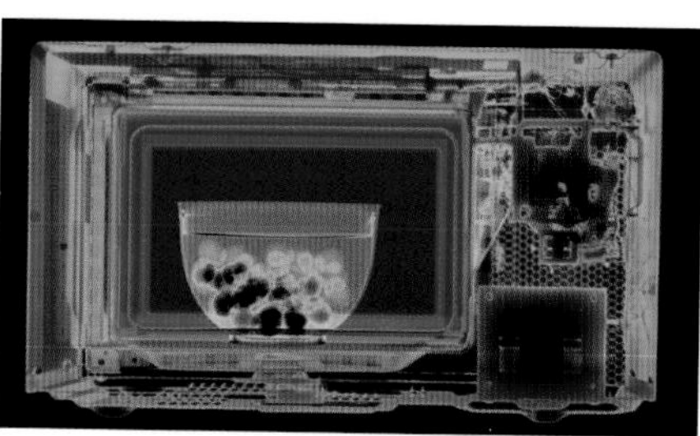

▲ **Microwave ovens**
As with many great inventions, the microwave oven was an accident. The inventor, Percy Spencer, was surprised to notice that, whilst standing near a magnetron (which generates microwaves), the chocolate bar in his pocket was beginning to melt. An avid foodie, he next tried popping popcorn kernels the microwave way before rushing to the patent office in Washington, DC, on 24 January 1950 to file a patent application for microwave energy to cook food (US Patent No. 2,495,429).

▲ **Diamonds**
Even diamonds may be the subject of patent protection. New laser technologies that micro-inscribe diamonds by graphitizing the diamond's surface are protected by patents.

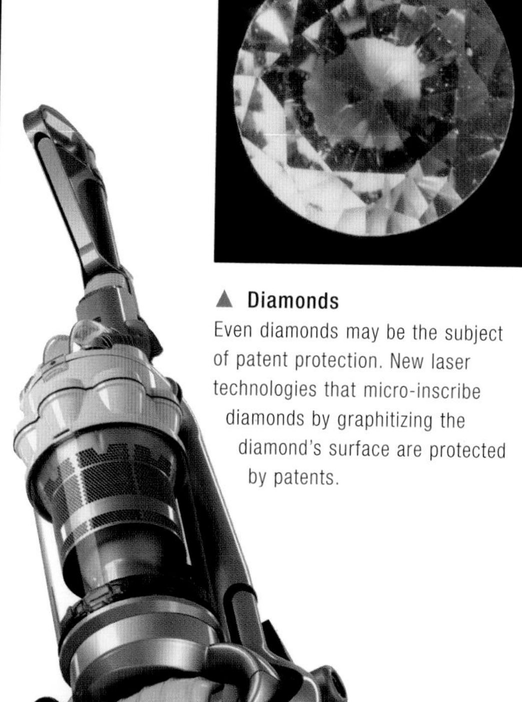

▶ **Vacuum cleaners**
Dyson's vacuum cleaner revolutionized the vacuum cleaner market by using G-force technology. No dust bag is necessary and all the dirt is collected in the cylindrical body. The centrifugal spin keeps the air stream clear, which means that there is a continuous, strong suction force.

Inevitably, we all want to pigeonhole things. It seems to make life easier. But it can restrict and hamper us. That said, here is a summary of categories covered in this book. Don't study it too hard at this stage – it is a starting point. When you finish the book, look at the chart again. Let the words and concepts flow together to create a whole – then you will be well on the way to using intellectual property to your benefit.



# summary

## TRADE MARKS

| Duration | What it covers | How to protect it | Tips |
| --- | --- | --- | --- |
| Indefinite as long as the trade mark is used. Trade marks often become your most valuable intellectual property after other assets have expired | Marks that identify and distinguish a product or service: **HEINZ**, **IPOD**, **LINUX**, the **MERCEDES-BENZ** star symbol, the **COCA-COLA** contour bottle, the shape of the **MORGAN** car, **DHL**, the name **ROBBIE WILLIAMS**, **DAVID BECKHAM**'s signature, the **ADIDAS** three stripes design | ▷ Through extensive use of the mark on your product or service<br>▷ Seriously consider registration with Patent and Trade Mark Office | ▷ Select a strong mark<br>▷ Keep records of use of the mark and especially the date of first use<br>▷ Obtain a trade mark search before use or filing to avoid disappointment and evaluate risk<br>▷ Consider adopting the same domain name or trade name as your trade mark<br>▷ Police and enforce your trade mark<br>▷ Use ® for registered and ™ for unregistered trade marks as warnings |

## COPYRIGHT

| Duration | What it covers | How to protect it | Tips |
| --- | --- | --- | --- |
| Life of the creator plus 70 years for most works | Works of art: literature, writings, computer software, visual designs, logos, photographs, website designs, music recordings, motion pictures, jewellery designs, architectural drawings | ▷ Automatic on date of creation<br>▷ Consider obtaining a US copyright certificate to assist in proof of ownership | ▷ Date and sign or stamp to show proof of ownership<br>▷ Consider obtaining notary, or third-party confirmation of date of creation, or statutory declaration<br>▷ Use a copyright legend as a warning: © 2007. John Smith. All rights reserved |

## DESIGN RIGHTS

| Duration | What it covers | How to protect it | Tips |
|---|---|---|---|
| Unregistered design rights: 10 years after first marketing of product but no longer than 15 years from date of creation. Registered design rights: 25 years from the date of filing | Ornamental shape of a product: design of a perfume bottle, the shape of a new car, ornamental necklace, distinctive packaging for a product, the shape of a biscuit, the shape of new handbag | ▷ Automatic on date of creation (unregistered design rights)<br>▷ Consider registering to help show proof of ownership (registered design rights) | ▷ Date and sign or stamp to show proof of ownership<br>▷ Consider obtaining notary or third-party confirmation of date of creation or a statutory declaration<br>▷ Consider a search before filing to avoid disappointment or huge expenses<br>▷ Don't disclose your design before filing |



## TRADE SECRETS

| Duration | What it covers | How to protect it | Tips |
|---|---|---|---|
| As long as the information remains confidential and is not disclosed or reverse engineered | Confidential business information: formulas, technical know-how, computer code, recipes, customer and supply lists | ▷ Keep it secret<br>▷ Have good practices in place to prove you maintain a secure workplace | ▷ Have business associates, subcontractors, and employees sign confidentiality letters or nondisclosure agreements to show proof of confidentiality |

## PATENTS

| Duration | What it covers | How to protect it | Tips |
|---|---|---|---|
| Twenty years from the date of filing patent application at the Patent Office | Inventions: telephones, light bulbs, online retail procedures, pharmaceuticals, certain computer programs, vacuum cleaners, ballpoint pens, the cut of a diamond, artificial heart valves | ▷ Through registration at the Patent Office<br>▷ Don't disclose your invention before filing | ▷ Run to the Patent Office to beat the competition<br>▷ Consider a patent search before filing to avoid disappointment or huge expenses<br>▷ Don't disclose your invention before filing<br>▷ Have everyone sign confidentiality letters or nondisclosure agreements until you are on file |

# bundling your assets



## TAKE A HOLISTIC APPROACH

The concept of bundling your intellectual property rights involves looking at your intellectual creation from a holistic perspective. You may have rights to more than one form of intellectual property, and these can be bundled together to help strengthen your arsenal. The more intellectual property rights you have established in your new creation, the better are the chances of an infringer being caught transgressing one of the boundaries. Believe me, in any intellectual property conflict you need strong and varied weapons – whether you are involved in the full-scale war of an infringement suit or the more subtle art of settlement negotiations.

The Panerai branded watch opposite provides an example of the different forms of intellectual property rights that may be embodied in a single creation (see pp.240-241 for more examples). You may wish to go through a quick checklist (see p.46) to see whether your new creation qualifies for protection in more than one category of intellectual property.

Q: How many forms of intellectual property do you think can be embodied in this watch?

A: There could be at least ten!

1
Design rights in the watch face design

2
Trade mark rights in the word mark "Panerai"

3
Trade name rights in the company name "Officine Panerai"

4
Trade secret rights in the manner of assembling the watch mechanism

5
Trade secret rights in the manner of manufacturing some of the parts

6
Patent rights in the crown lock mechanism

7
Design rights in the watch case design

8
Copyright in the design drawings of the watch

9
Copyright in the advertisements that feature the watch

10
Three-dimensional trade mark rights in the product design for the watch

## USE MULTIPLE LAYERS OF PROTECTION

The bundling of intellectual property rights is not a new idea. In fact, almost a century ago the **COCA-COLA** Company was already using the bundling strategy very effectively. On the advice of its intellectual property lawyer, the **COCA-COLA** Company developed the distinctive "contour **COCA-COLA** bottle" in 1915 in order to distinguish it from imitators and infringers in the marketplace. The **COCA-COLA** Company filed a "design patent" (akin to a design application), which protected the ornamental shape of the **COCA-COLA** bottle for a period of 14 years. Later on, the **COCA-COLA** Company was also able to protect the distinctive "contour" bottle shape as a trade mark. By this time, through extensive use, the shape of the bottle had acquired a reputation and identified and distinguished **COCA-COLA** in the minds of the average consumer.

In other words, the Coca-Cola Company bundled two different intellectual property rights in the contour bottle. This bundling strategy resulted in the protection of the shape of the bottle well beyond the original 14-year period.

HERE'S COKE . . . THE
PAUSE THAT REFRESHES
Coca-Cola
TRADE MARK REGISTERED
Coca-Cola
"Coke"
Ask for it either way . . . both
trade-marks mean the same thing.
5¢

# key tips



## 1 TIME IS OF THE ESSENCE

All intellectual property rights are time critical, so do not procrastinate. Follow the suggestions outlined in the different chapters to establish, as soon as practically possible, the relevant intellectual property rights in your creation. Where appropriate, take the necessary time and patience and follow the simple formalities outlined in this book to unequivocally evidence the first date of creation of your new intellectual property. So many intellectual property conflicts and cases boil down to one very simple issue – who was first in time and first in right. My advice to you is simple: run like blazes and beat your opponents to the post!

For some categories of intellectual property, you automatically get rights whether or not you formally get protection through the UK Patent Office. This applies to trade marks, where you can develop rights from use. And the same applies to copyright, where your rights exist from the moment of creation. So you might ask, why bother with registering these rights? Getting registrations helps pinpoint when you had what rights and what these rights are at a given moment. Also remember that a trade mark registration gives you nation-wide rights.

Even if your rights are prior to those of someone else, it is amazing how much money can be spent proving that you were first. And don't forget that fighting a dispute takes you away from your business. Filing trade mark applications for your important brands can save you lots of headaches in the long run. If your creation includes an invention, you have to get on file before any disclosures are made. Or you risk losing your rights immediately. So, especially with patent protection, it doesn't pay to delay.

## 2 DO NOT DISCLOSE YOUR NEW CREATION!

If you have come up with a new creation, you are proud, or excited, or enthused, or all of the above. You also want other people to try it out to see how they react or to make sure it works. But, if you are not careful with how you handle your new creation before you start filing and taking other precautionary measures, many of your rights could be at risk. As I have said before, this is not the time to show off. Save that for later.

Generally speaking, for virtually all forms of intellectual property my strong advice to you is to play things close to your chest. Do not allow someone to run away with your idea. This is particularly necessary when you feel compelled to discuss the concept or idea with someone orally. We all need sounding boards and protecting an idea or concept before it has been written down, or put into a tangible medium, is often very hard. But be professional: first go through the formalities of establishing your intellectual property rights, then have people sign nondisclosure agreements (NDAs) (see Appendix 6, pp.272-273), and only then can you start bouncing ideas off each other.

## 3 KEEP THOSE NOTES

Good housekeeping and good record keeping are essential. Obtaining and enforcing your intellectual property rights will often come down to producing the necessary evidence to convincingly demonstrate that you are "first in time and first in right". This is where the good note-taker always wins. You can almost never go wrong if you keep careful records from the date of inception and creation of your new intellectual property. Keep full and accurate records of all details that relate to the origination and continued use and development of your new creation.

# checklist



- ☐ Have you identified all the types of intellectual property that you hold? Are there any areas of crossover, for example a trade secret that could be patented, or a design right that could also be trademarked?
- ☐ Do you have the appropriate protection for your intellectual creations or business assets? Where possible, have you registered your intellectual property?
- ☐ Do your agreements with business associates, subcontractors, and employees clearly define the ownership of the intellectual property at stake?
- ☐ Do you have evidence to prove your ownership of your intellectual property? Are you keeping accurate records as evidence of ownership?
- ☐ Have you checked what your competitors are up to? Have you searched public registries and databases to see whether someone has filed or owns conflicting intellectual property rights?
- ☐ Are you making use of someone else's intellectual property in your own creations? If so, do you have the necessary clearance or consent?
- ☐ Are you policing your intellectual property to watch out for someone else infringing your rights?
- ☐ Have you used the appropriate warnings or notices to alert everyone to the intellectual property rights in your creations?
- ☐ Are you administering your intellectual property to ensure that the necessary rights are maintained and renewed in good time?
- ☐ Do you have the necessary safeguards in place to keep your creation confidential?
- ☐ Do you have good legal counsel who can guide you through all the above?

CHAPTER 1



# trade marks

## WHAT IS A TRADE MARK?

The alarm on your **ROBERTS** radio goes off. You turn on **RADIO 4** and you listen for a few minutes to **"THE TODAY PROGRAMME"**. You go into the kitchen, get some **STARBUCKS** ground coffee out of your **BOSCH** refrigerator and start brewing it in your **BRAUN** coffee maker with a **MELITTA** filter. While that's brewing, you

You have been up for 10 minutes and have already encountered scores of trade marks – words, slogans, logos, stylized letters, colours, package design, and even product designs that brand owners have developed and use to sell their products and services to you. You as a consumer have a choice as to which brands you want to rely on. What drove you to these – images, reputations, choice, happenstance, or habit? If you have any type of product or service that you want to sell, it pays to understand how to select, use, protect, and enforce

flip on your **SONY** television and check out **GMTV**. Next, you cut a slice of fresh **HOVIS** bread you got last night at **SAINSBURY'S** with your **SABATIER** knife and place it on your **HABITAT** plate (you are off the **ATKINS** diet this week). You sit down in your **IKEA** chair and start to review your email messages on your **HP** laptop. **YOU'VE GOT MAIL**.

your trade marks. The owners of the above trade marks have taken a lot of care and time doing this. So should you. A trade mark is a word (like **MCDONALD'S**) or design (like the **NIKE** Swoosh) or other indicator (like the **TARZAN** yell or the **TIFFANY** blue box design) used with particular products or services. A trade mark is the link between the manufacturer or service provider and the customer. It helps customers distinguish competing products and services from one another (like **VISA** versus **MASTERCARD**).

Once a trade mark develops a reputation, it will give the customer an idea of what to expect when they see that trade mark on new products and services.





Trade marks can also suggest a certain cachet (**HARRODS** v. **ASDA**). At the same time, trade marks can be used for any type of product or service, not just luxury or expensive items – think of **BIC**, the workhorse of pens, versus **MONTBLANC** and their finely crafted writing instruments. Once a trade mark develops a reputation, it will also give the customer an idea of what to expect when they see it on new products and services. Think of **BIC** disposable razors and **MONTBLANC** watches. It is more than the words that let you know what brands these are. The logos, typestyles, and other symbols all reinforce your comfort level with these products.

Trade marks also serve an important public interest: to help prevent consumers being deceived or misled into buying bogus products or services. When you buy a bottle of **BOOTS** aspirin for a headache, you expect it to work the same way it has for you in the past. But there are actually counterfeit drugs out there, and you would be very unhappy if you took a fake **BOOTS** pill that gave you liver disease.

Trade marks also serve an important public interest: to avoid consumers being deceived or misled into buying bogus products.

Unlike virtually all other intellectual property rights, trade mark rights last for as long as the trade mark is used – potentially forever! The UK mark for **QUAKER** oats was registered in 1894. Further, if your mark has been used sufficiently to acquire a reputation among the purchasing public, you are entitled to protection even in the absence of registration. But you need to keep using your mark to maintain these rights.

A patent covering a particular product may have expired long ago. But the trade mark for it lives on and can drive customers to that product instead of competing products. Many people would prefer to start off the day with **KELLOGG'S** corn flakes, rather than some other brand, even though the corn flakes patent expired long ago. No wonder a trade mark can be considered a more valuable asset than a patent.

We encounter trade marks or brand names from the moment we rise until we go to sleep every day. In fact, it is estimated that on average we see or hear more than 1,000 trade marks each day! It is not surprising that at present over 800,000 trade marks have been registered at the UK Patent Office.

> **TIP**
> **MAKE YOUR BRAND STAND OUT**
> In this crowded marketplace, anything you can do to separate and highlight your products or services from those of your competitors will pay off. Just look at the colour orange campaign of **ORANGE**. Do not underestimate how logos, slogans, colour, packaging design, sound, and even smell can be used to create a strong brand.



### Examples of trade marks

**HEINZ**, the **NOKIA** ring tone, the **MERCEDES-BENZ** star symbol, **LINUX**, **KARL LAGERFELD**, **HAVE A BREAK – HAVE A KIT KAT**, the shape of a **MORGAN** car, **DHL**, **ORANGE**, the name **ROBBIE WILLIAMS**, **HOOVER**, **PROZAC**, **RAY-BAN**, **HARRY POTTER**, **CHANEL**, **JAVASCRIPT**, the **TOBLERONE** triangular chocolate bar, **POWERPOINT**, **DAVID BECKHAM**'s signature, the **ADIDAS** three stripes, etc. are all trade marks.

### How are trade marks used?

Trade marks do not need to be restricted to a single product or service. They can cut across entire groups or categories of products (**JOHNSON & JOHNSON**) or, conversely, they can be very specific, like a style name (**FIESTA**). Even ingredients of products can be trade marks (**QUORN**). And what about business names and domain names? If they are distinctive enough and used in a certain way, they too can be registered as trade marks. Even if they cannot be registered as trade marks (and this is discussed further below), the law can still protect them.

Keep this in mind when you are selecting your brand. Do you want the brand to also be the name of the company (like **KODAK**) or a house mark for everything (like **CADBURY'S**)? Is it just a specific product name like **SPECIAL K** for a cereal? Will it be a style name like the **FOCUS** of Ford Motor Company, an ingredient for other people's products, like

**NUTRASWEET**, or will it be a domain name like **AMAZON.COM**? You may not know when you select the brand whether or not it is going to cross over and be used in these various ways. But it is not a bad idea to give this some thought.

## Not any old design or symbol is automatically a trade mark

It is easy to talk about trade marks we all know and recognize. But when a business is getting started or a particular product line is being launched, an important selection process occurs. Trade marks don't grow on trees! Instead, if it is done right, the trade mark will link the manufacturer or service provider to the customer base and will help customers come back to that brand over and over again. This is a lot easier said than done.

For example, does a customer recognize your trade mark as referring to your particular product or service alone? Does it enable customers to form an exclusive association with your goods or services? If the answer is yes, your mark is probably distinctive and you will be on your way to building a valuable asset. Some brand owners go for more descriptive marks because it immediately lets the customer know something about their product. Sometimes that works – you need to know your market and your customer base. You also need to know that descriptive marks are harder to search, register, and protect, and cost more to enforce.

# Does your trade mark enable customers to form an exclusive association with your goods or services?





## But any old word or symbol can become a strong trade mark if it is distinctive

You should not underestimate the types of trade marks you can use to build your brand. There has been a virtual revolution over the years. Now, colours can be used as trade marks if the owners put enough money and advertising behind them. Just look at the colour orange campaign of **ORANGE**. So do not underestimate how logos, slogans, colour, packaging design, product design, sound, and even smell can be used alone or in combination to create a strong brand. In this crowded marketplace, anything you can do to separate and highlight your product or services from those of your competitors will pay off.

## Examples of different types of trade marks

Word marks like **HEINZ**, logos like the **MERCEDES** star, sound marks like the **DIRECT LINE** jingle, packaging marks like the **COCA-COLA** bottle, colour marks like Day-Glo orange for **DYNO-ROD**, celebrity names like **TINA TURNER** and **DAVID BECKHAM**, character names like **MICKEY MOUSE**, and domain names like **ASKJEEVES.COM** are all trade marks.

## Only distinctive marks qualify

The essential function of a trade mark is to identify and distinguish the source of a particular product or service from other competing products or services. A trade mark must, in other words, be distinctive.

**DEFINITION** – Distinctiveness

Distinctiveness is a key concept in trade mark law, which not only helps determine whether your mark is registrable but also how weak or strong your mark is in enforcement proceedings against infringers. How distinctive your mark is essentially hinges on how much brand awareness it has, or is capable of evoking.

For example, when seeing your mark, will the customer recognize it as referring to your particular product or service alone? Does your mark enable customers to form an exclusive association with your goods or services? If the answer is yes, your mark will probably be considered to be distinctive.

## CATEGORIES OF MARKS

Armed with an arsenal of potential trade marks to create your brand or revitalize or update your existing brand, the selection process goes into high gear. What type of word will best help you sell your product or service? Is there an icon or logo to associate with your brand without even seeing the word mark (think of **MCDONALD'S** Golden Arches)? If you are a retailer or have an important product to sell, do you want your packaging alone to help sell the product without the consumer even seeing the label or name of the product (think of the **COCA-COLA** bottle)? At this stage of the game, the choices seem endless.

But all trade marks, unfortunately, are not created equal. Through evolution, trade mark law has come to recognize certain categories of marks to be distinctive or nondistinctive. For example, generic and descriptive marks are viewed as nondistinctive, while invented or fanciful marks are regarded as inherently distinctive. Suggestive marks fall in between. You should consider these categories, set forth below, very carefully when selecting your own mark. Think of them as candidates for a job interview. Some will be stronger contenders than others.

### 1. Generic marks (the slacker)

Generic terms refer to a category or type of goods or service. For example, the words "software, "jewellery", "furniture", "lawn mower", "coffee", and "credit card" can never be used to serve as a trade mark for a product or service of that category or type. The reason is obvious. Generic terms directly define the product or service itself and are not able to distinguish or identify its source. It is also essential to customers and the trade to be able to use such generic terms freely in order to compete effectively without anyone monopolizing these crucial terms. You should consider generic marks as the big no-no when choosing your brand name.

This doesn't mean you can't add a generic word to a distinctive word to create an overall trade mark, as in **SONY PICTURES**. Sometimes a generic word added to a distinctive word can help define your brand in the marketplace.

!

**NOTE OF CAUTION! –** Victims of their own success

Some famous trade marks have become victims of their own success. Trade marks such as "Cellophane", "Aspirin", and "Lino" have become so famous that customers have started using them to refer to the type of product. Therefore they no longer serve to identify and distinguish the particular manufacturer's products from competing products – they have come to designate the product itself. In other words, they have lost their distinctiveness. But take heart; there are ways and means to prevent this from happening when your trade mark becomes very famous. To avoid this, make certain that you have a good word to describe your product and keep it separate from the trade mark for that product. For example, you do not make a **XEROX**, you make a **XEROX** photocopy; you do not do the **HOOVERING**, you vacuum with a **HOOVER** cleaner. Your trade mark professional will be able to guide you safely out of the rough seas.

## 2. Descriptive marks (a weak candidate)

Descriptive terms help to describe goods or services or their characteristics. For example, **SOFT** for soap, **CLEAN-UP** for household cleaning products, **FRESH** for deodorant, **SMOOTH SKIN** for moisturisers, and **SHINY** for shoe polish all describe the goods or services in connection with which they are used. Descriptive terms do not help the customer to identify and distinguish a particular manufacturer's goods or services from those of his or her competitors. These terms are not usually registrable.

### Extensive use

There is, though, an exception to the rule that descriptive terms are not usually registrable. You may be able to convince a Trade Mark Examiner or a judge that your mark has lost its descriptiveness aspect as customers have come to associate the mark with you as the manufacturer through extensive use. You will have to produce persuasive evidence such as significant sales, advertising, and surveys over a period of time. This evidence will demonstrate that your mark has acquired a significant reputation. Your trade mark has come to symbolise the source of the goods, thereby identifying and distinguishing your product or service. Your mark has, in other words, become distinctive.

You can have a hard time protecting trade marks that are a surname, describe the location where your product is made, or sing the praises of your product.





Keep in mind that, even if your mark is eventually registered, it will in all likelihood be considered a weak mark in infringement proceedings against competitors. In my experience, judges are reluctant to deprive competitors of the right to use descriptive terms to describe their products or services.

**Laudatory terms** Laudatory terms, which praise a product in a direct manner (for example **BLUE RIBBON** for beer or **GOLD MEDAL** for flour) are also considered descriptive. Nondistinctiveness objections to laudatory terms can also be overcome only through proof of extensive use (for example, **IDEAL** in relation to rubber stamps and ink pads).

**Geographically descriptive terms** Geographically descriptive terms that truly suggest an association with a location (for example **CORNISH** pasties) are generally nonregistrable unless a significant reputation in the mark has been built up among the customers and it is possible to demonstrate that the requirement of distinctiveness has been met (for example **BOURNVILLE** for chocolate, **WATERFORD** for crystal, and **GRANADA** for cars).

### Examples of descriptive trade marks

Here are some good, strong trade marks we all know, but which were not born that way – **SLIMFAST** for diet products (descriptive), **TREAT** for

**TIP**

**WHAT IF MARKETING REASONS DICTATE I USE A DESCRIPTIVE MARK?**

In these circumstances, you will need to rely on long and extensive use to obtain your trade mark registration. This means that protection in the interim may not be straightforward. Therefore, I would also urge you to consider adding unique and significant graphics and other distinctive elements to your mark to build a composite mark, which may stand better chances of registrability and proper enforcement.

ice cream (sings praises), **BUXTON** for drinking water (geographic), and **SAINSBURY'S** for supermarkets (surname). Don't underestimate the amount of time and effort these owners have taken to protect these as assets.

**DEBUNKING THE MYTH** – It doesn't pay to get cute!

All too often I find that people believe that they can magically transform a descriptive term into a distinctive term if they deliberately misspell the descriptive term (for example "**FONE**" and "**XTRA**"), or if they contract two descriptive terms into one ("**TOYSDIRECT**"), use an unusual typeface (*"car-freshener"*), or add an internet domain name suffix (for example **SEVENDAYSAWEEK.COM**, **THEONEFORYOU.CO.UK**). Unfortunately, these quick fixes don't work and usually the Examiners are not amused.

### 3. Nondistinctive marks (an even weaker candidate)

Some marks simply lack distinctiveness and the reasons are various. Such marks don't identify and distinguish a particular manufacturer's product or service from those of its competitors. Once again, trade mark law has developed a number of categories of marks, which typically are presumed to be nondistinctive. These include:

- Long advertising slogans that may be too complex for the average customer to understand as identifying or distinguishing the product (for example **BRITAIN'S SECOND LARGEST INTERNATIONAL SCHEDULED AIRLINE**).

- A simple device mark, such as elementary geometrical shapes, that may be viewed by the average consumer as an illustration or ornament rather than a source identifier (for example the ubiquitous globe image used on so many international business products or services).

- Letters of the alphabet or short acronyms (for example **IT** or **ABC**) or numerals (for example **55** or **614**) usually lack distinctiveness unless they have gained a significant reputation with customers (such as "**501**" for jeans, "**No. 5**" for perfume or "**IBM**" for hardware). The same principle applies to bar codes, telephone numbers, internet addresses, times, dates, and technology standards.

- Common surnames, especially ones with long listings in telephone directories (for example **SMITH** or **JONES**), are considered nondistinctive unless the mark has become exclusively associated with a particular product or service (for example **ROTHSCHILD** for wines, **WH SMITH** for stationery).

▶ Marks that may deceive customers as to the quality, characteristics, or geographical origin of the goods are also considered nondistinctive (for example **COTTON-ETTE** for a polyester shirt or **CHAMPAGNE** for sparkling wine from Spain).

▶ State emblems or armorial bearings (such as royal warrants) or marks that are contrary to morality or public policy (such as obscene words or pictures) are also nonregistrable as trade marks.

### 4. Suggestive marks (good potential – the compromise candidate)

These are terms that are suggestive of the attributes or benefits of the goods or services but are not directly descriptive of the goods themselves. For example, **JAGUAR** for cars highlights the notion of "sleek, fast, and elegant", **DOVE** for soap evokes the idea of "soft and gentle", and **COPPERTONE** for sun-tan lotion suggests the much-desired colour resulting from using the product.

Other marks that fall into this category include names and letter combinations. Even though a surname is not automatically protectable as a trade mark, an entire name can definitely be protected from the beginning. For example, **RALPH LAUREN** was a good trade mark from the beginning.

Invented and fanciful marks are the heavyweights in the trade mark world.





Letter combination marks or acronyms can be good trade marks if the acronym itself has nothing to do with the product. For example, don't bother trying to use **TV** as a trade mark for televisions. But **HSBC** and **YMCA** were good marks from the beginning even if Hong Kong Shanghai Banking Corporation and Young Men's Christian Association would have been viewed as descriptive and not automatically protectable. Suggestive marks are typically judged to be distinctive by Examiners and often develop into strong marks.

### 5. Invented and fanciful marks (the star candidates)

These are words that are made up. They have no inbuilt meaning (for example **EXXON** for petroleum). Invented and fanciful marks are the heavyweights in the trade mark world. They are legally the strongest and most distinctive trade marks around. Their primary purpose to identify and distinguish your product from those of your competitors very well.

Invented or fanciful marks are typically new creations. Sometimes they are derived from a combination of bits and pieces of descriptive words for the product or service. Sometimes a computer spits them out. Sometimes they are words spelled backwards. Other times they are something that pops out of the head of a marketing genius. Examples include **ROLEX** for watches, and **KODAK** for photographic film. In the beginning, it takes some strong advertising effort to educate the

> **NOTE OF CAUTION! – Big resources required!**
> Although invented and fanciful marks can be very successful, it does take a serious commitment of resources and money to create brand awareness with customers in relation to these marks.





consumer to associate such trade marks with the products and services. But a good marketing campaign and, of course, a good product or service will get you a great and unique brand. Think of **GOOGLE** for the internet search engine.

### 6. Arbitrary words

This category is the source of many strong and protectable trade marks. These are dictionary words, terms, or phrases that are familiar to people but used for goods or services that have absolutely nothing to do with the product or service, for example **SMASHING PUMPKINS** for the name of a music group. These types of marks are automatically protectable. You will also have a strong mark that you can enforce against others.

Other marks in this category include made-up names. It is not uncommon for brand owners to adopt fictional names. For example, **UNCLE BEN'S** was a character name created by Mars, but it has become a strong trade mark. **WENDY'S** is derived from the name of the original owner's daughter. These are entirely good trade marks. Just make certain that you made it up and also that it does not belong to someone else who is already using it as a trade mark in your field.

Marketing experts much prefer descriptive or suggestive marks because they serve as a convenient communication tool.





**SO WHICH MARK TO SELECT?**

You have now come across the perennial dilemma, the tug of war, between trade mark professionals and marketing experts.

Marketing experts much prefer descriptive or suggestive marks. They will tell you that invented and fanciful terms convey no information to the customer about the product or service. Whereas, descriptive or suggestive marks immediately inform the customer about positive aspects of your product or service, and they serve as a convenient communication tool.

In the other corner is the trade mark professional. He or she will be keener for you to adopt a legally strong mark for both registrability and enforcement purposes, and will recommend the use of invented and fanciful terms and possibly suggestive words.

In my experience, the answer often lies in following the golden middle way: both marketing experts and trade mark professionals are usually able to work with suggestive marks. Suggestive marks are the compromise candidates, which often end up beating the star candidates to the post.

TIP

**OTHER WORDS AND SYMBOLS THAT ARE NOT PROTECTABLE**

Forget about famous marks, celebrity names, or titles. In this day and age when everyone is trying to stand out from the crowd, some people are tempted to adopt marks in this category. If you do that, you are wasting your time trying to register or enforce your trade mark. If you have a serious product or service you want to sell, please stay away from these types of marks.

### So which category of mark is best?

The answer is any category, except of course generic words. Think of **MONARCH AIRLINES** versus **BRITISH AIRWAYS. MONARCH** is an arbitrary mark. It would have been easier to protect than **BRITISH**, which is geographic. But after years of use and promotion, they are now both strong marks. That said, descriptive marks are probably the most common category of trade mark you will want to select. It is probably because you can immediately tell the customer about a particular feature, quality, or location of make of your product, or the person who designed it.

However, each commercial opportunity varies. Your product might compete in a market where the profit margin is low, and so is your budget. In these cases, you don't have the money or time to spend building a unique brand. You just need to make sales. On the flip side, you might be launching a new and unique item that will revolutionize the market. Or your company might be headed for an IPO. Here, you may have no choice but to adopt an invented or fanciful mark so that you can distance your brand from copycats, and impress your investors with a strong potential brand. When selecting your mark, choose wisely, taking into consideration all the pros and cons mentioned above.

In my experience, the answer often lies in following the golden middle way: both marketing experts and trade mark professionals are usually able to work with suggestive marks. Suggestive marks are the compromise candidates, which often end up beating the star candidates to the post.

Your trade mark professional knows descriptive marks are tough to protect and can prompt lawsuits by competitors. These marks need to earn their keep by being used carefully and promoted extensively. At the end of the day, it is your decision. You are the most familiar with your product and how you want to position it in the marketplace. Just because a particular brand might be difficult to protect does not mean it is a bad one.

Whatever words, logos, slogans, and designs you select, remember that it takes a serious commitment of resources and money to create brand awareness to educate the consumer. And, of course, the underlying product and service had better withstand the competition, or your brand will mean nothing to anyone, no matter how much time and effort you devote to brand selection.

### ▶ Don't use other people's names

Don't even think of using names, pictures, or other characteristics of celebrities or other living individuals as your mark, unless you are that celebrity or have their written consent. Your own personal name can be a very good trade mark. So can a made-up name. Ripping off someone else's name or image, like a fake Woody Allen voice to sell cars, is not going to get you anywhere except into a lot of trouble.

### ▶ Be careful with titles

Generally, titles of books, songs, albums, or movies are not protectable under trade mark law. But if you use them in a series, like **ROCKY I**, **ROCKY II**, and **ROCKY III**, *voilà*! You have trade mark rights. Or if you sell or give away merchandise under the title, you might be able to protect it, at least for the merchandise. Many West End show titles can pull this off, like **PHANTOM OF THE OPERA** or **LES MISERABLES**, when the mark is used extensively on merchandise.

### ▶ Don't use famous marks for other products and services

The owner of a famous trade mark can stop you from using the same famous trade mark, even if it is for different products and services. For example, you can't use **KODAK** for socks since **KODAK** is a famous trade mark. So don't bother trying to use a famous trade mark for your own products and services and then argue that your products and services are different from those of the famous trade mark owner.

Whatever words, logos, slogans, and designs you select, remember that it takes a serious commitment of resources and money to create brand awareness to educate the consumer. And, of course, the underlying product and service had better withstand the competition, or your brand will mean nothing to anyone, no matter how much time and effort you devote to brand selection.

## COMPOSITE MARKS

Once you have selected your mark, give serious thought to the idea of instructing a designer to develop a unique and distinctive picture, symbol, drawing, or logo device to become part of your mark. In conjunction, also consider using original, stylized lettering and unique colours or colour schemes. These different original and unique elements will all work together to help you create a distinctive composite mark which, in my experience, so often facilitates registrability. If you have succeeded in creating a truly composite mark, it may also qualify for copyright protection, in which case you are even more empowered to go after infringers (see chapter on copyright).

Look at the portrait of the Roman centurion on your **AMERICAN EXPRESS** card. Trade marks are not presented in black block letters on a white package with no background. Instead there is a whole supporting cast surrounding the word mark. If you are launching a new product or service or you want to rebrand your existing product line, think of using lettering, logos, slogans, distinctive colours, package design, and even product design. All these elements can be combined, and used consistently, to give your product or service a memorable brand identity. These are also trade marks that you can protect and own as assets. If you do it well, some of these supporting cast members will become stars on their own.

TIP

**TAKE A HOLISTIC APPROACH**

Whenever you are in the development stage with a new product and the way you brand it, take a holistic approach. Combining composite marks can help you create a distinctive mark, which will not only be stronger in the eyes of consumers, but will also facilitate registrability in law.



## Nontraditional marks

In recent years, the range of marks that may qualify for registration has expanded to some unusual and rather quirky areas. These marks are aptly named nontraditional marks. You should be aware of them because they may be relevant to your product or service. They include product and packaging design, colour marks, sound marks, olfactory marks, taste marks, gesture and motion marks, slogans, and logos.

### ► Product and package design

Generally, if you want to develop rights in packaging, the packaging has to be unique to begin with and it must be promoted as your trade mark for a long time. Packaging design can also be the subject of design rights. This way, you can try to get design protection while you are building up a reputation for the design as a trade mark. By the time your design right expires, provided you play your cards right, you will have developed a protectable trade mark in the packaging design.

However, if your product design has functional aspects, or if your consumers just don't think of the product itself as yours, forget about ever developing trade mark rights.

### Examples of packaging designs

Examples where rights have been developed in packaging include the shape of the **COCA-COLA** bottle, the shape of the **CHLOE** perfume bottle, the shape of the **MORGAN** sports car, the shape of the **JIF LEMON** bottle, the shape of a **SCRABBLE** tile, the **TOILET DUCK** disinfectant bottle, the shape of **CUSSON'S IMPERIAL LEATHER** soap. However, note that you cannot register as a trade mark a shape that is functional, for example, the **PHILIPS** three-headed razor.

▶ **Colour marks** Combinations of colour or a single colour may sometimes qualify (for example the Day-Glo orange colour for **DYNO-ROD** vehicles; the colour purple for the packaging of **CADBURY** chocolates; green and yellow colours for **BP** garages; the orange colour for **VEUVE CLICQUOT** champagne). It is very difficult for a single colour to qualify as a registrable trade mark and substantial evidence will be required to show the famous reputation of the colour in respect of the specific goods.

▶ **Sound marks** Audible and distinctive sounds (for example the sound of a dog barking for **ICI** paints; the **NOKIA** ring tone; the **WINDOWS** start-up tone; the **INTEL PENTIUM INSIDE** jingle; the **DIRECT LINE** jingle).

▶ **Olfactory marks** Distinctive fragrances (for example the strong smell of bitter beer for darts; the smell of freshly cut grass for tennis balls).

**TIP**

**COPYRIGHT**

Keep in mind that your design marks might also be protected under the copyright law. This gives you another layer of protection for your brand, and helps bundle up your rights. And if your designer is not your employee, make sure to get a written assignment of any copyright in the designs he or she creates for your brand.



▶ **Taste marks** The taste of foods; no one, so far as I know, has obtained a taste mark – so you can be the first – go for it!

▶ **Gesture and motion marks** Some gestures and motions have been registered (for example a man tapping one side of his nose with an extended finger for financial services).

▶ **Slogans** Think of **DON'T LEAVE HOME WITHOUT IT**. You know it stands for **AMERICAN EXPRESS** even without seeing that mark. It's a great slogan. And it also says something about the service – it's indispensable, it protects you. You can combine your own group of words to create your own slogans. Some slogans tend to be very descriptive, for example **SERVING YOUR COMMUNITY SINCE 1922**. This isn't the greatest slogan since sliced bread, but it does give consumers comfort that they aren't dealing with a fly-by-night outfit. And there is also a lot of pride in that message. Still, from a trade mark standpoint, it is not distinctive and you would probably need to stay in business until 2322 to protect it. If you are going to select a slogan, it's a good idea to spend time thinking about what you want to tell your customers about your brand every time they see it. If you are creative, you can also come up with a message that is so distinctive that customers will automatically think of your product when they see it. Such a slogan will be a protectable asset.

TIP

**SHIFT THE BURDEN**

Where possible you should file a trade mark application because once you have done this, the burden of proof on you is significantly alleviated. You no longer have to evidence that your mark has acquired a reputation through use – this is now presumed. The burden will be on your opponent to show that your mark is not valid. This is a significant advantage because it is not always that easy for your opponent to do this.





**Logos** Logos can be designs without words, word marks presented with stylized letters, or a combination of these. Some logos are designed so that the word portion and design portion can be used together and also separately. This is often done by stacking word marks and designs.

Or you can intertwine your word mark with a design. Some design marks become so well-known they are icons and you do not even need the word mark. Think of the red and yellow interlocking circles of **MASTERCARD** or the **PENGUIN** of Penguin Books.

!

**NOTE OF CAUTION! – Nontraditional trade marks**

A note of caution in relation to these nontraditional marks is required. They represent a relatively new and eccentric trend and Trade Mark Examiners, in my experience, treat them with caution. Keep in mind too that the old rules of descriptiveness and distinctiveness apply in these cases as well. For instance, if you wish to register the "unique" fragrance of your new perfume, this will normally be dismissed by the Examiner as "descriptive" of the product itself, i.e. the perfume. However, the "smell of roses" in relation to car tyres has been allowed, being considered "distinctive" for tyres and not "descriptive" of the product.

Judges and other authorities are impressed when you wave an official trade mark registration certificate at them. So obtain one if you can.





## HOW DO I PROVE THAT I AM FIRST IN TIME AND FIRST IN RIGHT?

Trade mark rights primarily flow from use. This means they are entitled to protection even though they are not registered. If you can demonstrate through use that your mark has acquired a reputation sufficient to distinguish your products – you have trade mark rights.

Where possible, though, you should seriously consider filing a trade mark application to register your mark. This will lift from your shoulders the burden of proof to show that your mark has acquired a reputation or is distinctive. This burden will now shift to the infringer to show that the mark *isn't* distinctive. In addition, you also have an official priority date earmarked – your registration date. The bottom line is that judges and other authorities are impressed when you wave an official trade mark registration certificate at them. So obtain one if you can!

### Keep good record of use

Trade mark rights essentially flow from use. The rule that applies is: "If you don't use it, you lose it". You have to evidence the fact that your mark is in continuous use. Therefore, as far as you can, try to keep a record of the date of the first use of your mark. "Use" in trade mark l aw means the manufacture and sale of the product bearing your mark.

The date of first use often becomes important in the time contest to show that you have a prior – and therefore stronger – right. The golden rule of "first in time, first in right" can really work in your favour in trade mark conflicts.

**NOTE OF CAUTION! –** Use it, or lose it!

If you don't use it, you lose it! If an opponent can show proof that you have not used your mark for a continuous period of five years, he or she can file a cancellation action for non-use. Always bear this time-sensitive rule in mind and keep up the good work by maintaining your records on the use of your mark. So that you can present evidence on the dates of use, you should:

- Preserve copies of invoices for your product or service.
- Keep accurate records of your sales and advertising.
- Keep accurate and dated notes of all meetings and discussions, including telephone conversations.

These records could be very useful in establishing your rights. The reason for this is that trade mark law requires you to prove that your mark has acquired a reputation through use. In other words, that it has become distinctive in the average customer's eyes and is used by the consumer to identify and distinguish your product or service. The burden is on you to prove that your mark has acquired a reputation

The date of first use is often important in the time-contest to show that you have a prior – and therefore stronger – right. The golden rule is: first in time, first in right.



through sufficient use. Good housekeeping with regard to keeping records of your trade mark use is highly beneficial.

### File a trade mark application

Filing a trade mark application with the UK Patent Office is of equal importance. This allows you publicly and officially to stake your claim in time before someone else does it. Once again, the golden rule of "first in time, first in right" can come to your aid. Moreover, you can file your trade mark application before you have even made use of your mark (although you have to have an intent to make use of your mark).

On a purely practical level, it makes a huge difference to judges and opponents if you are able to wave an official trade mark registration certificate at them in any conflict. But even if you do have such a certificate, continue to keep records because they always come in handy in trade mark disputes as proof of the strength of your mark.

## PREPARING YOUR TRADE MARK APPLICATION

### Trade mark searches: doing the groundwork

Before filing your trade mark application or using your new mark, it is prudent to have searches done at the UK Trade Mark Registry to determine whether someone else has already registered a similar mark. In other words, someone else may already be first in time and first in right. These searches are usually undertaken by trade mark professionals, but you may do some of your own searching online at the UK Patent Office (www.patent.gov.uk/tm/) to get some idea of what is already out there.

As outlined above, trade mark rights flow not only from registration but also, most important, from use. So, typically, trade mark professionals will also do a search to detect which marks, if any, similar to yours are already being used on goods or services (this is called a common law search). You may also want to take your own informal stab at this by typing your mark into Google or another major search engine, and seeing whether it reveals any conflicts. You may also wish to search any relevant online trade journals.

If the Trade Mark Registry search or the common law search reveals potential conflicts, your trade mark professional will assess how serious they are. After years of slugging it out in the searching trenches, I can tell you that this is one of the most difficult areas of trade mark law. I

**TIP**

**HAVE SOME BACK-UP MARKS**

The Trade Mark Registry in the UK and others around the world are becoming more and more cluttered. The chances are that of your choice will be eliminated or blocked by prior trade marks. Consequently, I would advise new trade mark users to pick more than one – three or even four– marks for a new product or service.



sometimes think more art than science is involved. Remember, you are trying to assess potential conflicts, which is a little like looking into a crystal ball. Essentially, you have to assess and predict who will decide to step forward and object to the adoption of your new mark. This is where experience really counts. Your trade mark professional will, when reviewing potential conflicting marks, basically assess two factors:

- How close the two marks are to each other, and

- How close the goods or services are in relation to which the marks are used (or for which they are registered).

**LEGAL TEST** – Are the marks similar?

The test is whether the average consumer is likely to confuse the products or services when confronted with the two marks, for example **BALLET** for footwear with **BALLY** for footwear, **CROSS BOW** beer with **STRONGBOW** cider. These two crucial factors will be judged in combination to assess whether someone else's mark could be potentially problematic.

> **TIP**
> **IT PAYS TO BE CONSERVATIVE**
> My suggestion would be not to be too greedy. I much prefer choosing a narrower, rather than a broader, description of goods. I usually find that Examiners are less inclined to raise an objection if you opt for the narrower description, and the chances of someone opposing your claim may also diminish. You can always file more trade mark applications to expand your description of goods or services as your business grows.

Trade mark searching helps enormously with the subsequent steps that follow after you have filed your official trade mark application with the UK Patent Office, namely, the Examination and possible Opposition to your mark. In fact, trade mark searches can help you anticipate potential obstacles and enable you to amend your application slightly before filing in order to avoid those potholes down the road.

### Classes

After a comprehensive trade mark search, your completed application should normally include details of your new mark and also the specification of the particular goods or services your mark will cover. There are officially recognized categories of goods or services (called classes) from which you must identify and select a suitable description of your specific product or service. (See Appendix 1, pp.258–263 for a guide to the different trade mark classes or www.patent.gov.uk/tm/reference/classguide.htm.)

Keep in mind that some products or services may fall into more than one class. For example, cigarette lighters fall into either Class 14 (goods in precious metals...) or Class 34 (smoker's articles), or both classes, depending on the material the lighters are made of. Protective clothing falls into Class 9, while ordinary clothing falls into Class 25.

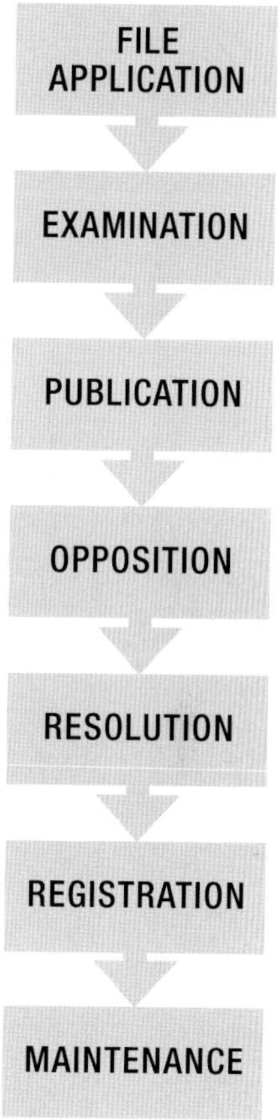

FILE APPLICATION
EXAMINATION
PUBLICATION
OPPOSITION
RESOLUTION
REGISTRATION
MAINTENANCE

## THE TRADE MARK APPLICATION PROCESS

So, now you are ready to file your trade mark application with the UK Patent Office. Once your application has been filed, you cannot change the ownership particulars (you either have to refile or transfer the trade mark, which can drive up expenses). Once you lodge your application, you receive an official application date and what follows next is the Examination and Opposition. Do not lose heart during these stages – patience and a cool head will stand you in good stead.

### Examination and Opposition: slings and arrows

Be prepared, the Examination and Opposition stages are nerve-racking and frustrating. Don't worry! This is normal. This period usually lasts about 4–12 months but sometimes can be longer.

**Official Actions** During the Examination phase an Examiner will communicate with you through Official Actions. He or she will, for example, cite prior trade marks, which in his or her view are too close to yours. The Examiner may also question the merit of your mark, commenting that it is "not distinctive" or "descriptive". Not to worry, these questions are bog standard normal. Most often they can be

**THINK ABOUT IN WHOSE NAME THE TRADE MARK WILL BE**

From long experience, I suggest you carefully decide in whose name the trade mark should be filed at this critical juncture from a financially efficient and tax perspective. For instance, should the mark be filed in your name or the company's name? You may wish to ask your intellectual property expert and read the chapter on x-ref below for more discussion on this point.





answered by clear and common-sense responses. Explaining succinctly why you are of the opinion that the mark won't be considered descriptive by the average consumer, or offering a revised and more limited description of your product or service will often do the trick. The key here, as in many other walks of life, is to communicate well with your Examiner. I find them to be very professional and courteous. Work with them, rather than against them. Call your Examiner or write to him or her.

Find out what the real concern is and address it head on in a constructive way. You may also request a formal meeting (a hearing) with a Hearing Officer, who is normally a senior official of the Patent Office.

**Publication** Once the Examiner is satisfied with your application, it will be published in the official *Trade Marks Journal* of the UK Patent Office. This means that the owners of prior trade marks will – within three months of publication of your trade mark application – have an opportunity to file an Opposition.

**Opposition** The owners of prior trade marks may oppose your trade mark application, usually on the grounds that your mark is confusingly similar to theirs. You and the opposing trade mark owner will be given timelines within which to file arguments and evidence to support your

The key is to communicate well with your Examiner.





cases. Your trade mark professional will typically build a compelling case for you by demonstrating that your mark (as well as the product or service in relation to which the mark is used) differs so much from the opposing owner's mark (and product or service) that the average consumer will not be confused. Help your trade mark professional as much as possible to find supporting evidence to build a persuasive case – hence the suggestions earlier to keep accurate notes of all advertisements, records, and minutes.

After all the evidence has been filed, the Examiner may decide the case on the documents before him, or decide to have an Oral Hearing. You are allowed to represent yourself at the Oral Hearing, or you may decide that this is a job best left to a trade mark professional or barrister. You and your trade mark professional should decide what will best suit your circumstances.

**NOTE OF CAUTION! –** Paying costs

You should be aware of one potential downside of losing an Opposition proceeding and that is that you may have to pay towards the opponent's costs. In other words, you may have to file a fresh application for a new mark and help pay the opponent's costs if you lose the Opposition. Carefully discuss all options thoroughly with your trade mark professional.

## IS AN OPPOSITION THE END OF THE ROAD FOR MY TRADE MARK APPLICATION?

No. Even if you run into difficulties in the Examination or Opposition stages, do not get discouraged. The fact is that a large majority of trade mark conflicts are settled by contact and communication with the owner of the potentially conflicting trade mark. For instance, at the Examination stage, it is standard practice to ask the owner of a prior trade mark (which the Examiner cited as an obstacle against your mark) to consent to your application. You will stand a better chance of obtaining the necessary consent by providing a few promises that you will, for instance, limit the use of your mark in relation to certain goods and not change your mark to move closer to the design of the prior mark.

When you encounter obstacles or oppositions, you can approach the other owner to work out a deal such as a consent or coexistence agreement (see p.87). Such agreements can help you get a registration if someone else has a similar mark, but they can be very dangerous if you do not know what you are doing. Also, expect people you approach to ask for money, a lot of it, and bargain from there.

Failing to obtain such an agreement is not necessarily the end. You may still be able to amend your application in order to overcome a citation during Examination or win an Opposition. Your trade mark professional can skilfully navigate you through these choppy waters.

**DEFINITION – Coexistence agreements**

A coexistence agreement is where parties agree to "live and let live". Typically, both sides agree to the use of their marks to certain goods or services only and use their respective trade marks in specific, different formats. (For an example of a coexistence agreement, see Appendix 2, pp.264–266).



### Registration and maintenance

Once you have overcome all obstacles to your application, you will receive your trade mark registration certificate from the UK Patent Office. This is a great day – treat yourself to a drink. You deserve it! It is important to note that the priority date of your mark dates back to your application date and not the date of registration.

And do remember to pay your renewal fees meticulously – the UK Patent Office will send you a reminder every 10 years, but do keep and rely on your own records because mishaps do happen and you may not receive the reminder. Please take extra care when paying any official fees to the UK Patent Office that you are dealing with the "real McCoy". Most unfortunately, there are a number of charlatan enterprises out there who may send you a bogus invoice that looks official but is not. Don't fall into the trap!

At this point, you have an asset that you can sell. You can use it to stop others from registering or using confusingly similar marks. And third parties will see your mark when they do searches. But you do need to continue to use your mark for the products and services listed in your registration or it can be attacked by someone. Don't warehouse or mothball your trade marks. Remember, if you don't use it you lose it!

**DEFINITION** – International

In the context of intellectual property, "international" here does not equal "worldwide". There is no such thing as a "worldwide" trade mark registration. Under the international Madrid system, you "pick and pay" accordingly. In other words, pick the countries of commercial interest to you and pay only for those countries' filing fees.





## REGISTERING TRADE MARKS OUTSIDE THE UK

With the expansion of the internet, more and more businesses are finding that they are trading with customers in Europe and the rest of the world. You may therefore find that you are using your trade mark in countries other than the UK. It is important to remember that trade mark rights are territorial, so, while a UK trade mark registration will protect your mark in the UK, protection will not extend to Germany, for example.

### Community trade marks

If you want to use your trade mark in other European Union countries, you can apply to a single registry, the Office for Harmonization in the Internal Market ("OHIM"), for what is known as a "Community trade mark" or "CTM". This simplifies the procedure, as you have to make only one application rather than applying to each country registry, which could save you money if you want protection in several countries, as you only have to pay one lot of fees. Once a CTM has been granted, your trade mark will be registered and protected in all countries of the European Union.

Further information about applying for and obtaining a CTM can be found on OHIM's website at www.oami.eu.int. Alternatively, your trade mark professional can fully advise you on applying and obtaining a

**TIP**

**TIME LIMITS**

Note that under the Madrid system, you must extend your "home" country registration to the other countries within six months. If you do this within six months, your original priority date will also be extended to other countries.



CTM. Once you have applied for your CTM, the application will go through a fairly similar procedure to that in the UK. However, it can be opposed by owners of earlier trade mark rights in any country of the EU, not just in the UK. The advice set out above relating to oppositions to a UK trade mark application applies equally to a CTM, and your trade mark professional will be able to guide you through the process.

## International trade marks

If you intend using your trade mark beyond the EU, you may want to consider filing for protection on an international basis. You can benefit from an international filing system that will allow you to file a single trade mark application and then extend protection in a large number of countries internationally. This is known as the Madrid system, administered by the World Intellectual Property Organization ("WIPO").

Your application for international registration, which originates in the UK (the "home" country), is carefully assessed for registration in all those countries you would like your trade mark to extend to.

Further details about WIPO and the Madrid system can be found at http://www.wipo.int/madrid/en/ and your trade mark professional will be able to advise you further about the procedure for obtaining protection internationally.

## LICENSING YOUR TRADE MARK

As the owner of a trade mark, you can always consider licensing your mark to others for the payment of a royalty. It is advisable to set forth the agreement between yourself and the licensee in a licence agreement.

**DEFINITION** – Licence agreements

Licence agreements are detailed agreements that grant third parties the limited right to use your brand (and that can include the word mark, logos, designs, and so on) for certain products or services in a certain geographic area for a certain period of time. In return, the other party will pay you some sort of royalty.

### Licence agreements

If you are lucky enough to own a brand that becomes popular, third parties might approach you to use the brand and all the imagery associated with it for goods and services they make. At one time, this sort of thing happened only in the entertainment and fashion fields. For example, the Walt Disney characters were heavily licensed. Now, there are licensing opportunities for all sorts of brands. Think of **JAMIE OLIVER** as a brand. This is where licence agreements come into play. But unlike copyright or patent law, trade mark law has a quirk, of which you should be aware when it comes to licences.

If you are lucky enough to own a brand that becomes popular, third parties might approach you to use the brand and all the imagery associated with it for goods and services they make. At one time, this sort of thing happened only in the entertainment and fashion fields. For example, the Walt Disney characters were heavily licensed. Now, there are licensing opportunities for all sorts of brands. Think of Jamie Oliver as a brand.

**EXERCISE QUALITY CONTROL**

You should make sure that you have the right to exercise "quality control" over the manufacture, design, and sale of the goods bearing your trade mark. After all, it's your brand's image that's at stake when you let others use it.



Typically, the licence agreement will contain clauses relating to the licensee's manufacture and sale of goods of a sufficiently high quality or standard. Again, the licensee will undertake not to place the trade mark in jeopardy by incorrect use. Furthermore, the agreement will state that the licensee will provide regular reports on the quantities of goods sold, the amount of money received, and the royalties to be paid. Further, the agreement could provide for the licensor to have a right to inspect the books of account of the licensee, or the premises where the goods are being manufactured.

## Quality control

The licensor and trade mark owner are required by law to exercise quality control over the licensee's manufacture and sale of the goods bearing the trade mark. The principle is simple: the trade mark owner stands behind the quality of the mark and should, therefore, keep an eye on the quality produced by the licensee.

Should you get involved in trade mark conflicts and need to prove that you have upheld the requirement of quality control, be fully prepared to do so. As a practical measure, I have found it helpful to formalize the status of someone, often an employee or subcontractor, who is already a de facto inspector of quality, by giving him or her the title of "quality control inspector" by way of a letter (see Appendix 3, p.267 for an example). The letter requires the quality control inspector to keep records of quality check inspections. Hey presto! You are now able to produce records and evidence of exercising quality control.

If you plan to go into the licensing business in a big way, it would be wise to have an employee dedicated to inspecting quality and acting as a go-between so that end consumers see a uniform image, whether the goods are made by you or by your licensee.

**NOTE OF CAUTION! –** Cancellation of registration

This is serious business. If you fail to monitor the quality of the products, a third party can cancel your registration or attack your rights in your mark for goods under licence.

The licensor and trade mark owner are required by law to exercise quality control over the licensee's manufacture and sale of the goods bearing the trade mark.

### Assignments

If you find yourself in a situation where you want to or need to sell your business, be sure to remember to think about your trade marks. If the buyer is buying all your assets and is going to carry on the business, he or she will expect you to sell your trade mark as well. But a trade mark is not just a word or other symbol. It has a reputation or goodwill associated with it. So any sale you make should include this. If the trade mark has been registered, you should schedule the trade mark on the sale agreement. However, in some instances you may not be selling the business and goodwill but just the trade marks – your sale will then be recorded "without goodwill".

Once that is completed, a simple assignment form can be recorded with the UK Patent Office. You should keep this in mind if you are buying a business as well – make sure you get the trade marks and the associated goodwill.

If you are buying somebody's trade mark but are not really buying the underlying business, don't get the false impression that you now own the brand. Sometimes people are willing to sell a trade mark as part of a settlement where they have alleged that your trade mark infringes their trade mark, or where you have approached them to work out a coexistence agreement.

Unless you also buy inventory, design blueprints, customer lists, and other assets that made the brand a trade mark and not a word, all you are doing is getting rid of this person as a potential problem. That may not be a bad deal. But just keep that in mind if you go down that road.

If you find yourself in a situation where you want or need to sell your business, be sure to remember to think about your trade marks. If the buyer is buying all your assets and is going to carry on the business, he or she will expect you to sell your trade mark as well. But a trade mark is not just a word or other symbol. It has a reputation or goodwill associated with it. So any sale you make should include this.

**IF SOMEONE COPIES MY TRADE MARK WITHOUT CONSENT, WHAT DO I DO?**

Your product or service bearing your trade mark is starting to take off through dint of hard work, plenty of resources, and expenditure of time. And then some freeloader comes along and has the effrontery to copy your trade mark. You are incensed that this person is stealing the fruits of your labour and capitalizing on the valuable goodwill symbolized by your trade mark. What to do?

If your products or services are sold through a sales staff or agents, they will often be quick to let you know about possible problems. After all, they are counting on your brand to make money and they don't want other people getting in their way.

It's a no-brainer if someone literally copies what you are doing. They are known as counterfeiters and the law provides some pretty clear steps on how to deal with them. But what do you do when someone starts using a trade mark that is identical to your own, but for different goods or services? Or worse yet, a rival starts to use it for competitive products and services?

Sometimes these people are purposely trying to rip you off, and other times it is just a coincidence. Either way, they might be infringing your trade mark rights and you can try to stop that. Sometimes you can even get money from them.

What do you do when someone starts using a trade mark which is identical to your own, but for different goods or services? Or worse yet, for competitive products and services?

But remember, having a trade mark right does not mean you own a word or design. Your trade mark rights come from the use of the words, logos, design, packaging, and other symbols you have built up as your brand in connection with your product line or services. So unless your trade mark is famous or an incredibly unique word, you are probably wasting your time getting upset about people using the same or similar marks in unrelated areas. Also, if you selected a trade mark from the descriptive category, it is going to be a lot harder to stop other people from using similar trade marks. Even if they are competitors. If someone starts to use a design mark or logo that looks like yours, you might also have a copyright claim. This is so even if they use it in very different products or services.

**LEGAL TEST** – The test for infringement

I suggest that you ask your trade mark lawyer to advise you on how best to tackle an infringer. But the first thing to ascertain is whether the imitator has in fact infringed your mark or whether you are overreacting. The test for infringement works as follows.

▶ **First in time** Crucially, you need to absolutely confirm that your mark is first in time and therefore first in right. The last thing you want to do is complain about someone else's mark when their mark precedes yours. They may very well turn around and send you a warning letter. Far better to let sleeping dogs lie in circumstances like these.

▶ **Likelihood of confusion** This is the benchmark for infringement of a registered trade mark. Will the average consumer be confused into thinking that the

## Warning letter: a shot across the bows

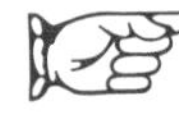

If your trade mark professional believes you have a case, you will typically be advised to send a warning letter. But be careful here, as UK trade mark law is very strict on this point. If you are considered to have made unjustified threats, you may face stiff penalties. So have your solicitor help you in drafting the warning letter.

If you are considered to have made unjustified threats, you may face stiff penalties. So have your solicitor help you in drafting the warning letter.





infringer's product or service emanates from the same source as the product or service bearing your mark? Factors such as the closeness of the marks (are they identical or similar? Are the products and services similar?) will be considered. In addition, direct evidence (unsolicited phone calls or letters from the public showing actual confusion) or indirect evidence (the proximity of the marks and goods) will also be relevant.

If your trade mark is unregistered, you will also have to prove that your mark has developed such a reputation and goodwill that consumers have come to associate your mark with your products or services. If you successfully cross this hurdle, you then also have to show that the infringer is likely to mislead consumers into believing that his or her product emanates from the same source as yours. He or she is passing off their product as yours.

The warning letter is a salvo shot across the infringer's bows and is meant to stop the infringer in his or her tracks. At this point, there is usually still room for a settlement. The settlement will usually require the infringer to amend or change the mark to make it less like yours. Failing a settlement, however, you will have to bring out the big guns and commence with legal proceedings, which are, sadly, very expensive and time consuming.

If you do nonetheless end up in court, chances are you will score some Brownie points with the judge for having made genuine attempts to settle first before litigating.





If you do get a response, don't be surprised if it's nasty. It is very rare that someone just backs down. However, many responses to cease and desist letters end with some sort of olive branch. Like, let's talk about it, even though I don't think there is a problem. That is usually a sign that you have someone willing to tweak their trade mark or maybe even phase it out if you give them some time. If you are interested in settling, go for it! If you do nonetheless end up in court, chances are you will score some Brownie points with the judge for having made genuine attempts to settle first before litigating.

If instead the infringer tells you to get lost or doesn't respond, you should either sue or walk away from the situation. Don't walk away and then change your mind years later – the courts will not be very sympathetic to you unless the infringer makes changes to worsen the situation over that time period. If you sue, expect substantial bills from your lawyer (unless he or she is your cousin or is doing it on a contingency basis). It is also useful to remember that in UK litigation, the successful party is usually awarded an order as to costs. This means that the unsuccessful party usually has to make a substantial contribution to the costs of the successful party. Also expect to have a lot of your time taken up answering questions, giving copies of documents, giving evidence, and basically being forced to spill your guts. Many people think this is a huge intrusion. But that is the way the system works.

It is also useful to remember that in UK litigation, the successful party is usually awarded an order as to costs. This means that the unsuccessful party usually has to make a substantial contribution to the costs of the successful party. Also expect to have a lot of your time taken up answering questions, giving copies of documents, giving evidence, and basically being forced to spill your guts. Many people think this is a huge intrusion. But that is the way the system works.

**TIP**

**ENFORCE YOUR MARK**

Whatever you do, make sure you look at watching service reports regularly, like once a week. Don't let them sit around or you can miss important deadlines. Besides, the sooner you put someone on notice about your rights, the more likely you are to settle with them.





If your mark is slavishly copied (almost identically copied) on similar products, in other words, being counterfeited, you may seek the assistance of Customs, Trading Standards, or the Police, who may seize the counterfeit goods for you.

## Enforcing your mark

Again, unlike copyright or patent law, trade mark law has a unique requirement that you should be seen to police and enforce your mark. In other words, you should actively fend off infringers and preserve the exclusivity of your mark. If you do not, and you allow your mark to become diluted by permitting similar marks to be registered or used alongside yours, the Patent Office and the courts will probably not help you if you decide later on that you would like to stop new imitators from registering or using marks similar to yours. In a sense, you will have lost the effectiveness of your trade mark rights by allowing them to become diluted.

**Watching service** You should seriously consider subscribing to a watching service, for example, www.cpaglobal.com. These will keep you informed of trade mark applications that may be too close for comfort to your mark. You may then – depending upon the merits of each case – decide to oppose the specific application (see Opposition, p.84). Equally,

if you stumble across someone using a mark similar to yours, discuss the case with your trade mark solicitor.

## SO YOU HAVEN'T REGISTERED YOUR MARK. WHAT'S NEW?

Do not fret. You can still protect your mark if it has not been registered, provided you can meet a few requirements. A special category of law called "passing off" (or "unfair competition") has developed over time.

**DEFINITION** – Passing off

The rules of passing off do not allow someone to misrepresent his or her goods as the goods of another. A trader is not allowed to compete unfairly by trading on the reputation and goodwill of someone else's trade mark. In other words, the law enables you to take action against someone who rides on your reputation.

Essentially you need to prove:

▶ That your mark has developed a sufficient reputation and goodwill for consumers to associate it with your goods or services.

▶ That the interloper is misrepresenting to consumers that his or her goods or services emanate from your business, to the extent that confusion is likely to arise.

▶ That you are likely to suffer damage as a result of the confusion – but generally the court will hold that damages will follow if confusion has been established.

Do not forget that, even if you do not register your mark, it is highly advisable to determine whether you are infringing someone else's prior trade mark. In other words, before you adopt a new mark, have your trade mark professional do searches to assess your situation.

However, it is always advisable and preferable to file and obtain a trade mark registration. The reason for this is very simple. If you take legal action on the basis of a passing off action, the burden of proof is on you to demonstrate the three points mentioned above.

However, if you are able to wave a trade mark certificate at your opponent or in a court of law, the burden of proof shifts to your enemy. Your opponent is now obliged to prove that your mark is not distinctive – in other words, your mark cannot distinguish your goods or services. So my motto is always: when in doubt – file!

Your trade mark lawyer will show you how best to demonstrate these points convincingly.

### OTHER CORPORATE CHANGES SUCH AS MERGERS AND NAME CHANGES

It is wise to record these with the UK Patent Office. Otherwise, there will be a great deal of confusion if you want to sell your brand, or if you want to rely on your mark in an infringement case.

## Security agreements

Just as you get a mortgage on your house, a bank will sometimes loan you money if you pledge your trade marks as collateral. Some banks use old forms that make you assign your rights to them. That doesn't make any sense! They should not own your trade marks because they do not know how to run your business. You wouldn't sell your house to them in return for a mortgage, would you? Then why would you sell your trade marks to them in return for a loan? Most banks have got their act together over the years.

> **NOTE OF CAUTION! – Mortgages**
>
> If you are thinking of obtaining a licence for a trade mark, for example to sell video games under a particular entertainment property, or to sell the perfume of a well-known clothing designer, find out whether the the company has mortgaged its trade marks. If it has, and if it goes bankrupt, the court can terminate that licence and you could be left holding the bag!

### Customs recordals

You can record your trade mark registration with UK Customs. Then Customs agents located at airports and ports will be on the lookout for counterfeit products coming in from other countries. Customs will seize and destroy counterfeit products and also assess fines against the importer. It is difficult to know how many products they really catch, but in recent years they have become far more vigilant. You want Customs on your side: they are there to help you.

### Trade groups

There are a number of coalitions and other trade associations that have banded together to go after counterfeiters in particular industries. This helps keep costs down. Also, counterfeiters do not pick on just one brand. They do a lot of different stuff. So this is one time when you want to get along with your competitors – you all have the same problem, and I encourage you to get involved.

Customs will seize and destroy counterfeit products and also assess fines against the importer.

Trade names serve to identify and distinguish one business enterprise from another. Consequently, they often overlap with trade mark protection.





## TRADE AND COMPANY NAMES AND INTERNET DOMAIN NAMES

I would like to draw your attention to two related areas of law that overlap with trade marks. They are trade and company names and internet domain names.

### Trade names and company names

If the business under which you sell your products or services is incorporated as a company, you should give serious thought to adopting the mark you have registered, or used in relation to your products or services, as your company name and trade name as well. Trade names serve to identify and distinguish one business enterprise from another. Consequently, they often overlap with trade mark protection.

Even if your business is not incorporated, you may still wish to use as your trade name the same mark you use for your product or service. **COCA-COLA**, **NESTLE**, **MARS**, and a number of other famous brand names have done just this. There is a distinct legal advantage to doing so. In some trade mark disputes, the additional umbrella of protection provided by trade names turns out to be quite useful. Trade names may assist with priority dates (especially where a company or business has operated under that name for a long time). Trade names may also support evidence of use or reputation insofar as they overlap with your

**TIP**

**SEARCH FOR THE BEST DOMAIN NAME**

It gives you a significant marketing advantage if you own a domain name that is the same as your brand name. While you are searching the Trade Mark Registry for your new mark, also check whether it is available as a domain name. In fact, these days I am in the habit of checking domain name availability first, when dealing with brands that need to be visible on the internet.





trade marks. In a nutshell, the bundling of trade names and trade marks has, in my experience, been helpful in trade mark conflicts.

### Internet domain names

Domain names have quickly become an extremely useful tool to help promote brands. Websites at the addresses for these domain names can also be used to sell product or give information on it. The internet is like a big billboard showing up on everyone's desk, laptop, and PDA. Just think of **AMAZON.COM** in the field of books or **LASTMINUTE.COM** for travel. If you manage to get a domain name which corresponds to your trade mark followed by ".com" you have a terrific edge in the marketplace.

Domain names are an extremely useful tool to brands. Just think of **BURBERRY.COM**, **JAGUAR.COM**, **BA.COM**, and a host of other brand name sites. Without even making use of a search engine first, I intuitively visit these sites by typing the brand name followed by ".com".

If you have a domain name that is the same as your brand name, you have a significant marketing advantage and are able to attract customers directly to your real-world shop window through cyberspace.

If you end up having a popular brand, expect to encounter pirates who get domain names which are similar to your marks.





If you have a domain name that is the same as your brand name, you have a significant marketing advantage and are able to attract customers directly to your real-world shop window through cyberspace... This gives you a terrific edge in the marketplace.

It is very easy to check the availability of domain names yourself. Here are a few websites that offer the service free:

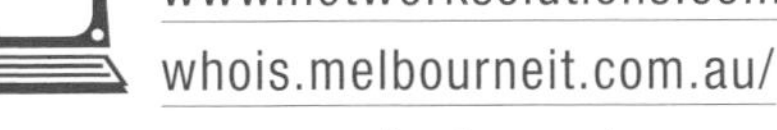

www.networksolutions.com/en_US/whois/index.jhtml

whois.melbourneit.com.au/

www.nominet.org.uk

If your preferred domain name is not available and you cannot change your trade mark and brand name, do not despair, as there are other solutions:

▶ You can always adopt a domain name that incorporates your brand name but with a suitable prefix or suffix such as "emark" or "markonline". The chances are that these combination word marks will still be available.

▶ You can check whether a domain name you need – but which is already registered by someone else – is in fact actively used. This can be checked on sites such as www.centralops.net/co/.

If the domain names are not actively used (and sometimes even if they are) you should give thought to approaching the owner with a polite request to purchase the domain name. You can obtain his or her contact details by looking up their "**WHOIS**" details at a site such as www.networksolutions.com/en_US/whois/index.jhtml.

Stories abound of domain name owners fleecing those who wish to purchase their names from them. But it is my experience that most owners are quite reasonable in their asking price – especially now that we have entered calmer waters after the dotcom boom-and-bust era.

If your preferred domain name is not available and you cannot change your trade mark and brand name, do not despair, as there are other solutions.

You may just come to a sensible and reasonable arrangement – it is definitely worth a try.

Another development that has received a lot of press is the practice of domain name pirates who register the names of famous people or businesses before selling them back to these individuals or businesses at a steep profit. Recent court decisions have tended to frown upon these so-called cybersquatters.

Another development that has received a lot of press is the practice of domain name pirates who register the names of famous people or businesses before selling them back at a steep profit. Recent court decisions have tended to frown upon these so-called cybersquatters.

**HOW SHOULD YOU DEAL WITH PIRATES?**

If you end up having a popular brand, expect to encounter pirates who register domain names that are similar to your marks. How do you deal with these? Some companies go after everyone, whether the website is active or not. Other companies selectively and methodically pursue the pirates who have active websites or who are trying to sell the domain names. I think this latter approach makes a lot more sense. You certainly do not want to encourage the pirates. In fact, there are now dispute resolution procedures in the UK as well as around the world that can be followed and, if successful, can force a pirate to transfer the domain name registration to you.

Keep in mind that, if you are already the owner of a registered trade mark or company name, you may be in a position to prevent someone else from registering your mark as a domain name. If the person have acted in bad faith and the domain name is confusingly similar to your mark, you may have a good shot. There is an expedited arbitration procedure to assist with domain name recapture. For more information on this practice, you may wish to look at, for example, www.arbiter.wipo.int/domains/index.html. Although this procedure is relatively quick and not too expensive, you should ask your trade mark lawyer to assist you.

# CHAPTER 2 copyright

## WHAT IS COPYRIGHT?

Stop reading for a moment. Look up. Look around. What do you see? Are there **POSTERS** or **PAINTINGS** on your walls? Are you wearing a **PIECE OF JEWELLERY** with some ornate inscriptions? Do you have a **FANCY TATTOO**?

The truth is, we are surrounded by paintings and other visual art, writings, software, dance, music, film, and other artistic creations where someone has expressed themselves in some sort of medium. And all these expressions may be protected by copyright from the instant they were rendered in a tangible medium of expression.

The moment you use your own ingenuity to create an original story, a poem, an article, a painting, a drawing, a song, or even software, you automatically have copyright in your creation. While large media and entertainment companies such as motion picture studios,

What about the **PATTERN** on your clothes – is there anything special about it? And if you are watching **TELEVISION** (I discourage multitasking while reading my **BOOK** by the way), what about the **TELEVISION PROGRAMME**? Is it a **SITCOM**? A **MOVIE**? The nightly **NEWS**?

record labels, advertising agencies, and publishers rely on copyright protection, so can you. Use your ideas and create something real with them! If you are a writer, a visual artist, a web developer, a graphic designer, a songwriter, a photographer, a musician, a movie producer, a comedian, a performer, a choreographer, or any other creative person, you need to know that your ideas are automatically protected under copyright law the moment you express them on paper or record them in some other fixed format. But you should also make sure that other people know it's your creation and find out what to do if someone copies it or uses it without your permission.

TIP

**KEEP IT TO YOURSELF**

Because you need to get your ideas down on paper, it's not a good idea to tell your friends or family or anyone else about what you have in your head. Telling someone about something does not give you any copyright. If someone takes one of your ideas and writes them down before you do, you are out of luck. We all have ideas. It is getting them down onto paper that's tough. And it's that sweat equity and creative spirit that the copyright laws are there to protect.

Copyright covers works of art in the broadest sense. Originally it was intended to provide protection to traditional art forms such as literature, music, sculpture, and paintings. Today, however, copyright has been extended significantly to embrace, among other things, creations such as computer software code, distinctively designed websites, "format rights" in television game shows, and uniquely designed logos. The reach of copyright is therefore very broad indeed.

### Further examples of copyright

Copyright can, for instance, include architectural drawings, the layout and design of an internet web page, jewellery designs, radio and television broadcasts, motion pictures (including DVDs), sound recordings (including CDs), motorcar designs, photographs, dress designs, play scripts, sculptures, magazine or journal articles, and engineering drawings. Copyright also exists in computer source code, including virtually every single piece of software running on your computer – from your operating system to your word processing programs to your internet browser. Copyright, however, does not normally cover names, titles, and slogans, but these may be protected as trade marks.

Even though the list of what copyright can protect seems like it would cover everything under the sun, it does not. Copyright protection does

Even if your "creation" ends up not being protectable under copyright law, you might be able to protect it with an unregistered or registered design or maybe even a patent.



not necessarily apply to "useful articles". It is not always easy to tell whether an article is just useful or has some sort of artistic merit where the copyright laws kick in. Most clothing designs and even many jewellery designs are not protected under copyright laws. At the same time, fabric patterns used on dresses and highly ornamented jewellery pieces can be protected under copyright.

Even if your "creation" ends up not being protectable under copyright law, you might be able to protect it with an unregistered or registered design or maybe even a patent. Or if you use and promote it a certain way for a long time, you might even be able to protect it under trade mark law.

### Express yourself: copyright protects the physical expression of ideas

Take your ideas and create something real with them! I cannot stress enough how important it is to get your ideas out of your head and onto paper or your hard drive. The moment you do that, you have a creation or a "work". And as usually happens, once the idea is out of your head and onto paper or into your laptop, other ideas start to flow and the work begins to grow and develop. Your new creation might not be a Picasso painting or a Tom Stoppard play or a John Lennon song. But it's yours to develop, keep private, sell, or exploit however you wish. With some talent, ingenuity, marketing, and a lot of luck, you might have a valuable asset. And if someone copies it or uses portions of it, he or she will have violated your copyright, which can lead to a lot of trouble.

It is important to note that copyright can exist only if it has been rendered in a tangible medium of expression. In other words, merely having a light bulb go off in your brain and carrying a fantastic idea around in your head are not enough. You have to express it tangibly. Write those fantastic ideas down on paper so that you have it in black and white, or create your graphic designs utilizing computer software. There must be some physical rendition of your work that can be viewed over time. It is very important to understand that copyright serves to protect only the physical expression of ideas and not the ideas themselves. Ideas are like the air, sea, and land – free for all to use. It is copying the specific expression of these ideas that is *verboten.* When people cut corners and do wholesale copying of words, musical notes, and graphics (i.e. plagiarizing a work that is in tangible form), they get into trouble.

There must be some physical rendition of your work that can be viewed over time.

**NOTE OF CAUTION** – Don't disclose your ideas

Keep your new and original ideas to yourself until you have rendered them into a physical format (and established your rights as more fully described below). If you discuss these ideas with an unscrupulous colleague, for example, and he or she writes them down before you do, you will have been beaten to the post. Remember first in time, first in right? You may have thought of the idea first, but it is only when your idea is in tangible form that you can start running.

## Copyright protects original work

Your "work" must be original. It must emanate from you and not be copied from someone else. Just as no one can copy from you, you cannot copy from someone else if their work is still protected. Your work should represent your own fresh, unique interpretation of the subject. Obviously, we are all influenced by the world around us, so anything you create will inevitably have influences from the outside world. But there is a big difference between that and copying.

Interestingly enough in theory, copyright does recognize the fact that two individuals who are located at opposite ends of the globe may – independently of each other – create more or less the same work. In such a case, both creative spirits will own copyright in their respective works because they were created independently and are original.

Moral rights belong only to you and cannot be transferred to someone else.





**Copyright: the right to stop copying**

Copyright, as the word itself implies, gives the exclusive right to the owner to copy his or her work. This exclusive right to copy the work includes the right to stop others from reproducing your protected work. You can also stop others from creating derivative works, spinoffs, or translations of your work. You also have the right to stop others from selling, displaying, or performing your work without your permission. This economic right entitles you as the owner to stop unauthorized copying by someone else. Apart from the economic right, you as the copyright owner have moral rights.

**DEFINITION** – Moral rights

Moral rights protect the way in which your work or creation is used or attributed to you. Moral rights belong only to you and cannot be transferred to someone else (except your estate). For example, if you are the author of a work or a book, you have the right to be identified as the author. You can also use your moral rights to object to derogatory treatment of your work. For example, if you are the composer of a piece of music, you have the right to prevent it from being used in a contentious television programme or in a jingle for products you would not want to be associated with.

In some cases, moral rights may even allow you to stop the mutilation of your artwork, even if someone else owns the actual physical work, in order to protect your moral rights and reputation. So what does this mean? The other person might own the physical object with your work but you still own the copyright and moral rights in the actual creation. For example, selling an original painting or piece of jewellery or sending out a copy of your book manuscript or TV show proposal does not mean you give away your copyright.

It is prudent to retain a copy – digital or otherwise for record purposes – of your work when you sell a physical object, such as a painting.

### What is the lifespan of copyright?

Copyright lasts for the life of the author and for 70 years after the death of the author or creator for most works. Sound recordings, computer-generated works with no human author, and broadcasts are protected for only 50 years from the date of the creation or publication.

## HOW DO I PROVE THAT I AM FIRST IN TIME AND FIRST IN RIGHT?

I have always found it fascinating how many copyright cases turn on formalities and on proving that you are in fact the owner of the work in question. Demonstrating that you are the rightful owner often forms the nub of a copyright conflict. Surprisingly few copyright cases hinge on whether there is infringement or "substantial copying".

### If you created it, it's yours

Note that copyright automatically vests with the owner upon creation. If you created it, it's yours. There are no formalities to comply with or requirements to fulfil in order for you to register your work or to use a copyright notice. Simple, isn't it?

### Make sure you can prove it's yours

However, from long experience I can tell you that, from an evidentiary perspective, it is crucial that you are in the best possible position to prove that you are the owner of a particular work. If you've created it, it's yours. But go the extra mile and make sure you can prove it's yours. Steps you can take to ensure you are in a strong position to evidence your ownership include dating and signing your work, using a copyright legend, a stamp or seal, a notary, a statutory declaration, or a US copyright certificate.

Demonstrating that you are the rightful owner often forms the nub of a copyright conflict.



**1. Date and sign** As a first step, I suggest that you automatically date and sign (with your own signature) the bottom of each page or document (in hard copy) or, if in another medium, at the end of the work. If your work is in electronic format such as source code, I suggest you provide your name and the date of creation – together with a copyright legend – at the beginning of your code. Some software programs already date stamp documents automatically, which will be of additional assistance.

**2. Copyright legend** Together with dating and signing the work, you should also consider adding the international copyright legend along the following lines:

© 2007. John Smith. All rights reserved.

In other words: © followed by the year of first publication and then the name of the owner plus the words "All rights reserved", which provides you with some international extension rights. This legend serves the useful purpose of warning other people that you are claiming copyright on this work.

**3. Stamp or seal** It is prudent to also have either a stamp or seal made up incorporating the following wording:

> *I, John Smith, confirm that*
> *I am the author of this*
> *design, which is an original work*
> *Signed* ________________
> *Date* ________________

Obviously, the word "design" in this legend should, if necessary, be replaced with another word such as "software program", "book", "musical composition", or a more general descriptor, for instance "work", depending on the nature of the copyright work involved.

**4. Notary** The above-outlined measures will undoubtedly assist you in proving the ownership of your work. However, courts are understandably reluctant to rely on such evidence alone. In view of the rampant forgeries and fraudulent practices judges have to deal with on a daily basis, they are generally sceptical of unverified statements. Consequently, it makes for sound practice to have the statement contained in your stamp verified by an independent third party such as a notary. The date of creation of the work is the most important fact, which the notary will verify. For this to work most effectively, the verification should take place as soon as possible after the stamp has been affixed to the work (or drawing thereof in case of designs). The notary should use language along the following lines:

> *I hereby certify that this document was presented to me bearing the above stamp today [insert date].*
> *Signed ________________*
> *Notary Public*

The Notary Public statement should preferably appear just below your stamp. In the case of works rendered in electronic format where digital signatures by you and the notary are not possible, you may wish to print out the work and affix your stamp and the notary's statement at the end.

In view of the rampant forgeries and fraudulent practices judges have to deal with on a daily basis, they are generally sceptical of unverified statements.

In some instances, such as design drawings or sketches, many versions of the same subject may be produced before a final one is chosen. If this is the case, you may want to limit using your stamp and the accompanying notary statement only on the version of the end of each work session to save time and expense.

**5. Statutory declaration** Instead of the stamp and accompanying notary statement, you may wish to attach a statutory declaration to the end of your work or relevant documents. For an example of a statutory declaration, see my website www.fromedisontoipod.com.

**6. US copyright certificate** Another quite useful method I have found to help verify the date of creation and ownership of a work is to try to obtain a copyright certificate from the US Copyright Office. The reason for this approach is that one cannot register a copyright work in the UK. You can do this, however, in the US, which is one of very few countries where you can register and obtain a copyright certificate. Although such a copyright certificate is an official US document, it may be useful to present as additional evidence of ownership in the UK and elsewhere. In order to file a copyright application in the US, you should take the following steps.

### Steps for obtaining a US copyright certificate

▶ Fill out the copyright application form of the US Copyright Office found at www.copyright.gov.

▶ Pay the application fee (currently US$45).

▶ Submit the application form and the filing, together with a copy of the work, to the US Library of Congress, as more fully explained at www.copyright.gov.

**NOTE OF CAUTION** – Official Actions

A copyright application is not automatically accepted. You may receive a query (called an "Official Action") from the US copyright Examiner. The comments are usually straightforward and can often be answered on common-sense grounds.

If successful, you should receive your certificate of copyright registration approximately six months after filing. Keep in mind, though, that the registration is effective from the date of receipt of your application at the US Copyright Office.

An additional benefit of a US copyright registration is that, if you are ever required to enforce your copyright in the US, there are some significant advantages that flow from registration:

▶ Copyright registration is required for filing a lawsuit in the US if the copyright owner is a US citizen.

▶ You are eligible for both statutory damages and lawyers' fees, which amount to sizeable numbers, if an application to register your copyright work was filed before the infringement occurred. The mere fact of having the registration often results in a quick settlement, without protracted litigation, when the infringer knows that he or she is faced with paying both his or her own legal fees and yours.

**NOTE OF CAUTION! –** Filing an application in the US

You should be aware of a potential downside to filing a copyright application in the US. If your application is rejected in the US, and you wish to extend and protect your work in the US at a later time, you may encounter difficulties. So, if in doubt whether your work is worthy of copyright registration or if you require assistance with the US copyright registration procedures, you may want to consult a US copyright lawyer on this point.

Keep in mind that most copyright works filed with the US Copyright Office are publicly available.





Also keep in mind that most copyright works filed with the US Copyright Office are publicly available. If you file a work that is confidential, for example computer source code, the US Copyright Office permits, on written request, a redacted version of the work to be filed in support of the application.

For a selection of copyright lawyers go to: http://www.martindale.com/xp/Martindale/Lawyer_Locator/search_advanced.xml and type in "copyright" in the "specific area of practice" field together with the desired location.

**DEBUNKING THE MYTH** – The closed envelope myth

I would like to debunk an "urban legend" that is bandied about as a tip to help you prove the date your work was created. Time and again I have come across the unshakeable conviction that if you post your work to yourself, provided the envelope remains unopened, the official date on the postage stamp will be considered irrefutable proof of when your creation was conceived. Envelope tampering is common, however, and when you're in court and the chips are down, this form of proof may be considered dubious at best.

TIP

**KEEP RECORDS**

Ensure that you keep safe custody of all your copyright records. Good housekeeping is paramount. For truly important works, you may consider keeping a second set of records at a different location in case of fire, flood, or other damage.



## Assignment

Since your copyright is actually a bundle of rights, like holding a bunch of sticks, always remember that you can sell or give permission to use some of these rights to one party and keep the other rights for yourself. You can sell or license these rights to someone else. This gives you a lot of flexibility with your rights. But keep good records of exactly what rights you are giving up and make sure who has them, for what purpose, and for how long. If you read the preceding sections, you will appreciate why this is important.

Copyright as intellectual property, not unlike tangible property, can be bartered, bought, sold, inherited, and transferred in whole or in part. For example, you can assign the right to translate your magazine into a foreign language while retaining the copyright in the English language version. An important fact to keep in mind is that copyright ownership can be transferred, or assigned, only if the agreement to assign is in writing. Also remember that, if you sell your sculpture or painting, you retain the copyright in that work. This has several implications.

**Magazine articles** If you write an article for a magazine, you still own the copyright in the article unless there is an agreement to assign the article to the magazine publisher. By submitting the article for publication in the magazine you do, however, provide the magazine publisher with an implied licence to publish your article. However, if you are employed by the proprietor of a newspaper or magazine, the copyright in that article would belong to the proprietor of the magazine.

Copyright as intellectual property, not unlike tangible property, can be bartered, bought, sold, inherited, and transferred in whole or in part.

**Commissioning** If you hire or commission a subcontractor such as a photographer or a graphic designer, don't assume that you can use their work in perpetuity wherever and whenever you wish. If you hire and pay a freelance photographer to take photographs for your book, or if you commission a graphic designer to produce designs for a computer program that you are compiling, the photographer and designer will automatically own the copyright in the photographs or designs, unless you reach agreement to the contrary. In other words, it is very much in your interest to negotiate a once-off fee for their work and to obtain a written assignment of their copyright (along the lines of the copyright assignment agreement in Appendix 5, pp.270–271), so that you will then own and be able to exploit the copyright. If you do not obtain an

When hiring a subcontractor, it is prudent to negotiate the price and assignment up front in order to prevent a renegotiation of the price later.





assignment of the copyright, you may well run into problems with the subcontractor when you come to use his or her work, as he or she could request further fees from you. The position could be even more complicated where you wish to sue a third party for infringing what you believe to be your corporate logo, since the design agency may be the actual copyright owner.

On the other hand, if you have been commissioned to produce a work of sculpture or to design an album cover, you will want to try to retain the copyright or at least negotiate a good price for an assignment. Try to find out how your work may be exploited in the future, so that you can agree on the appropriate figure.

When hiring a subcontractor, it is prudent to negotiate the price and assignment up front in order to prevent a renegotiation of the price later. If this was overlooked, don't despair, you may still be able to obtain the assignment at a later stage. In such a case you may prefer to call it a "confirmatory" assignment and make it effective as of the date of creation. If you are unable to obtain an assignment from the photographer or designer, you may still be allowed to use their photographs or designs. You may rely on the fact that there is an implied licence to use the photographs or designs for their intended purpose. Licences may be oral – unlike assignments, which must be in writing (exclusive licences, though, also have to be in writing). However, be very cautious, because any new or expanded use, such as a reprint of the book or new edition of the computer program, will exceed the scope of the permissible use. Such use may be beyond the scope of the original project and accordingly the implied licence.

**Websites** A problem that all too often arises in this context is the development under contract of websites. For the reasons outlined above, making sure that you obtain from the website designer a copyright assignment of his or her website design is highly recommended in accordance with the suggestions mentioned above. For an example of an assignment agreement, see Appendix 5, pp.270–271.

**Commissioning versus employees** In some instances, the subcontractor's work may not qualify as a "commissioned" work. This is typically the case where the subcontractor is your employee and has created the work in the ordinary scope of his or her employment, for example a graphic designer employed to specifically create book covers. The work then belongs to you as the employer. Even here, and in other situations where the "commissioning" principle applies, it is still prudent to record in writing the agreement you have with the subcontractor on the ownership of the copyright.

## Licences

As the owner of a copyright work you always have the option to license someone else to copy and distribute your work for the payment of a royalty. It is advisable to set forth the agreement between you and the licensee in a licence agreement (an exclusive licence must be in writing).

I cannot stress enough how important it is to know that you can also license out all or any portion of your copyright. These licences can be given on an exclusive or a nonexclusive basis and they can be given out for varying lengths of time. It is a little like renting out rooms of your house to different people for different purposes.

While such nonexclusive licences do not need to be on paper, I strongly urge you to get them in writing. This way, everyone knows what they are getting. Also, the termination rights that apply to assignments also apply to long-term licences, whether exclusive or nonexclusive.

Under a licence, you can collect royalties. If you do that, make sure you know what the standard in your industry is – it varies. Also, you should find out exactly how the royalties are calculated and when they are due.

You can also license out all or any portion of your copyright under licence. These licences can be given on an exclusive or a nonexclusive basis and they can be given out for varying lengths of time. It is a little like renting out rooms of your house to different people for different purposes. While such licences do not need to be on paper, I strongly urge you to get them in writing.

In fact, it may be useful to include in your licence agreement the fact that the licensee must prepare regular (for example, quarterly) reports on sales, coupled with the royalties due, together with an audited financial statement at year end showing the total financial position. You should also make it clear exactly which rights you are giving out and for how long. If you are giving out the right for your play to be performed, you should make it clear whether the performance is for a single stage performance or a performance that is broadcast over television or turned into a film. All these rights can be divvied up into as many pieces as you like. You just need to make it clear when you are entering into your licences what you are giving out.

If you are taking a licence from someone with a copyright work, make sure you know what you are getting in writing. If the licence is nonexclusive, the author is allowed to give out the same rights to someone else. You pay a lot more for exclusive rights, but you should understand that when doing the deal.

Types of licences that you should be aware of include "open source licences" and "Creative Commons licences".

▶ **Open source licences** Not everyone wishes to benefit financially from their creations. There are some admirable creative spirits who prefer not to earn any money from their works but to donate it to the public good for the benefit of society.

An example of this is the "open source movement" of software programmers. These programmers make their source code freely available by way of an "open source licence". In practice, what this comes down to is that the end user may make copies of the software without payment. The "open source licence" does not, however, operate on an anything goes principle. Any modifications and improvements made to an open source work, or secondary works derived from the original work, require the creator to distribute the modified work on the same free basis as the original open source software. It truly is the gift that keeps on giving.

The Linux operating system, which is well-known for its superior stability and security aspects, is an example of an "open source licence" (www.opensource.org).

Not everyone wishes to benefit financially from their creations. There are some admirable creative spirits who prefer not to earn any money from their works but to donate it to the public good for the benefit of society.

▶ **Creative Commons licences** A similar system to open licences, which also promotes the use of copyright in order to encourage the creative reuse of intellectual works, is advocated by the Creative Commons movement (www.creativecommons.org). Creative Commons licences are not designed for software but for other kinds of creative works such as music, film, photography, literature, and website designs.

With a Creative Commons licence you can allow other creative spirits to copy, distribute, display, or perform your work or derivative works without charging a royalty. This can, for example, be done on the condition that you are given credit or that your work is used for noncommercial purposes only. For example, Cindy publishes a photograph of herself on the web using a Creative Commons licence. She is keen for everyone to use her photograph, provided she receives credit. John downloads her photograph, displays it on his website, and gives her credit. And everyone is happy!

Creative Commons licences allow other creative spirits to copy, distribute, display, or perform your work or derivative works without charging a royalty.

**TIP**

**FIGHTING INFRINGEMENTS**

If an infringement occurs, don't start getting excited about getting money out of the infringer. If you think someone has stolen your copyright, remember there might be some arguments on the other side. The opponent might say the use is a "fair use", or that you do not have a valid copyright, or that your work is not original, or that you have given permission. So expect a long and protracted battle unless your opponent made a clear error.

## IF MY COPYRIGHT WORK IS COPIED WITHOUT CONSENT BY SOMEONE ELSE, WHAT AM I TO DO?

You have slaved over your intellectual creation. It has cost you many sleepless nights and often substantial financial outlay working on some sort of software program. Or one of your paintings is finally accepted in an art show. Then you realize that someone else has copied your work without permission. What are you to do?

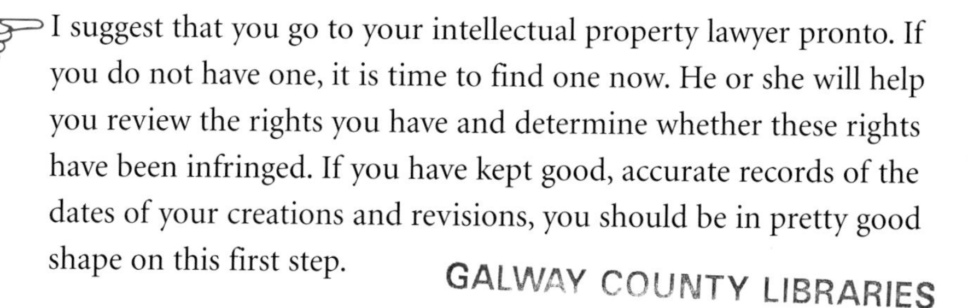

I suggest that you go to your intellectual property lawyer pronto. If you do not have one, it is time to find one now. He or she will help you review the rights you have and determine whether these rights have been infringed. If you have kept good, accurate records of the dates of your creations and revisions, you should be in pretty good shape on this first step.



You will have to prove that the work in question is substantially similar to yours. This, like almost everything else in the law, is open to interpretation. Someone does not need to copy your entire work to infringe it. Taking relatively brief excerpts from a book or including one of your paintings in a photograph used in an advertisement can be an infringement. Creating a work based on your work is also an infringement of your rights.

Someone to whom you have given a certain right in your work can also be an infringer if they use the work for other purposes. For example, selling someone your oil painting does not give him or her the right to produce posters of it. And creating a little icon for a single ad doesn't give someone the right to adopt it as their logo on every item they sell for the next 50 years. These are different rights that you still have.

**LEGAL TEST** – Substantial copying

The guideline for infringement of copyright is whether there has been a "substantial copying" of the original work. Unfortunately, this standard is open to interpretation and there is no bright line definition to determine whether what has been copied is trivial or substantial. As these cases are thorny, you may wish to consult a copyright lawyer on this issue. Expert guidance is usually required to embark on the complex procedures necessary to stop someone from copying your work or to sue for damages. Once it has been determined that substantial copying has indeed taken place, you will typically be advised to send a "cease and desist" letter to the infringer. This is a shot across the infringer's bows and is meant to stop the infringer in his or her tracks. At this point, there is usually still room for a settlement. Failing a settlement, however, you will have to commence with legal proceedings, which are expensive.

Works in the public domain comprise the body of all creative works and other knowledge considered to have become a part of society's cultural heritage.



## HOW DO I MAKE SURE I'M NOT INFRINGING SOMEONE ELSE'S COPYRIGHT WORK? STAYING OUT OF TROUBLE

The creative process is a plant that requires constant nurturing. It is important for creative spirits to be able to reach even greater heights by standing on the shoulders of the giants who have preceded them.

In some instances, you are free to copy and rely on other original works when composing your own. You may copy works that are in the "public domain", copy subject matter that will qualify as "fair use" or "fair dealing", copy ideas rather than the specific expression of the ideas, or obtain "clearance" or "consent" to copy a particular work.

### Public domain

Works in the public domain comprise the body of all creative works and other knowledge considered to have become a part of society's cultural heritage. These iconic works may therefore be used and copied without permission and payment of a royalty.

For instance, *Turner*'s paintings and *Byron*'s poems are in the public domain but not the paintings of *Andy Warhol* and *Picasso* or the songs and records of performances of *Elvis*. Usually works become part of the public domain because their intellectual property protection term has reached the end of its lifespan. Examples of works in the public domain

TIP

**REMEMBER THAT LAWS VARY FROM COUNTRY TO COUNTRY**

This means that a work in the public domain in the UK may not be in the public domain overseas. If you plan to distribute your work outside the UK and unless you are absolutely certain that the work you copied is in the public domain around the world, you need to check on a country by country basis. Even big companies have tripped up on this one.

where copyright has expired include the plays and verses of *William Shakespeare*, the works of *JS Bach* and the **MONA LISA**. Unless it is obvious that the copyright in a work has reached the end of its term, you should contact the publishers or agents or heirs of the author's estate to confirm this fact or consult a copyright lawyer to be absolutely sure.

Also watch out when using texts that seem at first blush to be part of the common cultural heritage – such as classical Greek texts or *Tolstoy*'s **WAR AND PEACE** – as the translator of these works will hold the copyright to the translation. Works that do not attract copyright protection, such as noncreative works, may also be in the public domain, for example mathematical formulas and facts.

The book **THE WIZARD OF OZ** by *L. Frank Baum* is in the public domain, but the classic *Judy Garland* film by *Warner Brothers* is actually different from the book. All that additional material in the *Warner Brothers* version is still protected by copyright law.

Remember the basic tenet of copyright? The expression of the idea is protected, not the idea itself.



Determining whether something is in the public domain is tricky. As I mentioned before, there might be works that you believe to be in the public domain that actually embody or include new material. I already gave the example of **THE WIZARD OF OZ** but there are numerous other examples where the work you are most familiar with is still protected under copyright law.

### Fair use

Fair use, or fair dealing, provides leeway to those engaged in noncommercial research, private study, professional criticism, the review and reporting of current events ("newsworthy items"), and teaching in schools. For example, provided a sufficient acknowledgment of the author and the source is given, students writing a dissertation can consult and copy articles and small sections of works; a literary critic can copy sections of a novel when reviewing it in an article; a journalist can quote from a company's financial report in a news bulletin. This is a rough guideline and you may wish to consult a copyright expert to ensure that you are on safe ground in the case of these permitted exceptions. Remember the basic tenet of copyright? The expression of the idea is protected, not the idea itself. Copyright subsists in the specific expression of ideas in a tangible medium. Therefore, if you express someone else's idea in your own words, you should be able to do so.

**NOTE OF CAUTION! – Take care when using others' works**

Take care. Do not cut corners. Do not copy large tracts of text (in the case of literary works) or segments (from designs or graphic works). If you do so, you are in breach of copyright because you have stolen the expression of the idea instead of simply making use of the idea. It will leave you open to infringement claims.

True, there are no hard and fast rules. But I always advise clients to completely avoid copying any specific words or design or graphic elements and, when in doubt, to listen to their inner voice. If it doesn't feel right, it probably isn't. This is the area where copyright and plagiarism principles often coincide.

For example, nothing prevents you from writing a children's book around the idea of a school for wizards. However, if you copy tracts, wording, or segments from *JK Rowling*'s **HARRY POTTER** books, in other words, substantially copying the expression of her work, you would infringe her literary creation. For example, purchasing a CD, DVD, or book does not give you the right to make a copy of the content, even though it may be for private use only. Equally, downloading from the web, electronically scanning, or merely photocopying a work are all "copying". Be careful.

If you need to copy a work that still enjoys copyright protection, I suggest you consider obtaining clearance or consent from the owner of the copyright. This is a very common practice, especially in literary works where people often quote brief extracts from the works of other authors.

The old saying that "possession is nine-tenths of the law" does not work when it comes to copyright law.





### Clearance or consent

If you need to copy a work that still enjoys copyright protection, you should consider obtaining clearance or consent from the owner of the copyright. This is a very common practice, especially in literary works where people often quote brief extracts from the works of other authors. You will almost always have to do this if you wish to quote poetry.

Sometimes it is relatively easy to track down the owners of the copyright. Start by getting in touch with the author's publisher or agent. He or she will usually be able to help you or they will refer you to the author's lawyer, who will assist you in obtaining a permission to make use of the work (such as a quote) for a certain sum of money, usually not an unreasonable sum. I suggest that you seriously contemplate following this route and that you make sure you keep an accurate record of all your permissions and consents. These will normally be granted for a certain period of time or a certain number of copies. You may be granted permission to use the extract for the first printing of your book. Any subsequent reprints will require a renegotiation of the permission.

You may also decide to opt for obtaining the necessary consent from some organizations representing groups of copyright owners, which may be able to offer you a licence to use copyright material. Examples include the Copyright Licensing Agency (CLA) for authors and publishers at

www.cla.co.uk, the Designers' and Artists' Copyright Society (DACS) for visual arts in the UK at www.dacs.org.uk, and the National Music Publishers' Association (NMPA) for musical works at www.nmpa.org.

It is also quite helpful to go through associations such as these when you have developed a "derivative work" from an existing work. For example, if you have translated a work or dramatized a novel or made a photograph of a painting or an arrangement of a musical work, your creation will be a "derivative work". Identifying the creator of an existing work for permission to adapt it to a "derivative work" on which you are working might not always be easy. I suggest you contact the appropriate society such as the ones mentioned above.

If you need to copy a work that still enjoys copyright protection, you should consider obtaining clearance or consent from the owner of the copyright. This is a very common practice, especially in literary works.

> **TIP**
>
> **POSSESSION IS NOT NINE-TENTHS OF THE LAW**
>
> You should be aware that the old saying, "possession is nine-tenths of the law" does not work when it comes to copyright law. Remember, copyright is a bundle of rights. There are rights in the physical original. There are rights to make copies. And there are rights to create new works based on your existing work, such as a sequel of a book, a recording of a song, or a poster of a painting.



## MAKING SURE EVERYONE KNOWS WHO HAS WHAT RIGHTS

Giving someone a right to use your work doesn't give them all rights. Selling your original canvas painting to someone does not give them the right to make posters or calendars or stationery of it. And giving a magazine the right to publish your story doesn't give it the right to produce a movie with it. The same applies to software. While many CDs come with limited licences, you should know the terms before you start making copies. Be careful! Just because it's easy doesn't make it lawful.

### Photography

A photographer owns the copyright in his or her photographs. The photographer does not own the subject matter, so if you want to take your own photograph of the same object, that's fine. A skilled photographer takes into account many factors when taking pictures. It is not just the push of a button. This means that if you hire a photographer to take pictures at your wedding you cannot just run off on your own and make as many copies of these pictures as you wish. That is a violation of the photographer's copyright. You need special permission, and will probably pay an extra fee for that. The same applies to photographs that are given to advertising agencies. Unless it is a commissioned work and it is agreed in writing that copyright will belong to the commissioner, or the photographer assigns all the copyright, the photograph is given for only a specific

When you buy a CD, you are not buying just a piece of plastic; you are buying the end product of a lot of people who have put their creative expression into it.



purpose. Commissioning happens when, for instance, a photographer has been asked by another person to take the photographs. A photographer who gives a photograph to an advertising agency for an ad shot has not given up the right to use it for posters or on packaging. If you are a photographer, make sure all this is sorted out when you are hired for a job, so that everyone knows what they are getting out of the deal.

### Music

In the music field, there are "compulsory licences" available for songs. You pay a certain amount of money in return for permission to use a song. But don't confuse getting permission to use a song with permission to use a particular recorded performance of the song. There is a separate copyright in the performance. Performances of certain songs have become a rich source of music in advertisements over the years. A lot of money changes hands, so make sure you understand the rights you are getting and you have negotiated for before moving forward.

By now, I hope you understand why the recording industry and everyone else associated with it go nuts when people copy or download recordings and pass them along to others without permission. A lot of time, effort, and money go into finding the right artists, selecting their

TIP

**COMMISSIONING ARTISTS**

If a commercial artist is hired for a major project, it makes sense to have him or her assign all their copyright for a fixed fee (although they will want to retain the right to use and copy the work for their portfolio and to show others what they can do). It is in the interests of both parties to get all this straightened out before work begins.

good songs, getting the recordings of their performances made and engineered so they sound just right, and then getting them on to a CD or other piece of software. When you buy a CD, you are not buying just a piece of plastic; you are buying the end product of a lot of people who have put their creative expression into it. And that is all protected by copyright. If you are a musician, a songwriter, or a sound engineer, you know that already!

### Commercial artists

If you hire a graphic designer or other commercial artist to create an advertisement, a booklet, or even a website, make sure you know what you are getting for your money. If you are a graphic designer or commercial artist, you want to make it clear to your clients what they are getting and what they are not getting for the fee they pay. You should also negotiate with them up front what it would cost to assign all your rights to them versus what it will cost to licence out certain additional rights. No one should assume that for a small payment they can use a creative work forever or for any purpose. The last thing anyone wants is to have a graphic designer sue them. And the last thing a graphic designer wants is to go after a client. That's not good business.

But if it is after the fact and you discover that you need additional rights from a commercial artist, you can try to negotiate an assignment or additional licence at that time. If you get an assignment, you can call it a "Confirmatory Assignment" and make it effective as of the date the artist created the work (for an example of a copyright assignment agreement see Appendix 5, pp.270–271).

!

**NOTE OF CAUTION!** – The internet

The internet is a magnificent research tool and provides no end of interesting, quirky, fresh material. Even though the prevailing culture on the internet is free-wheeling and rather anarchic, you may not copy these materials for your own works, no matter how seductive they are. Despite their mass distribution and availability (easily downloaded), these materials are typically not in the public domain. For instance, even small icons and logos may be works of art and copying them might constitute copyright infringement. There may, in fact, be many copyright works contained in a single web page: text (literary work), graphics (artistic work), and sound files (musical work), for example. Exercise caution. Just because the medium is different does not mean the principle is.

**NOTE OF CAUTION!** – Copyright of website designs

A problem that all too often arises is who has what rights in a website developed under contract. If you are having a website built, make sure that you obtain a copyright assignment of the website design from the website designer. If you are a web designer, make sure the client knows which rights are included in your fee.

## Computer programs

A computer program is considered to be a literary work. This means, for instance, that if you download a computer program from the internet, store it on a web server, run it on your PC, or display graphics of the program on a monitor, all these activities will, usually, amount to "copying". Conversely, when you develop your own website it would be a good idea to mark each page with the international copyright legend (see p.125) together with information on whether you are happy for others to use your material with or without your consent.

**NOTE OF CAUTION!** – Databases

You should also be aware that databases are protected by copyright if their selection or arrangement of the subject matter is original. In addition, databases may also be protected by a separate "database" right if a substantial investment of time or money went into developing the database, which lasts for 15 years from the date of creation or, if it is published during that period, 15 years from the date of publication.

> **TIP**
>
> **WEBSITE LINKS**
>
> Instead of copying material from another website, you may wish to create a link to it. Although you may not be copying, you might be considered to have authorized others to copy material from that website. Also, your link may be viewed as "framing" (linking to a site as a frame within your own site) and you may be violating trade mark and passing off law. I suggest you seek permission from the webmaster of the site you wish to link to. People are usually keen to have links to their sites because this leads to more hits.



### Giving credit

Sometimes you may feel that, by citing an author when you've made use of his or her work, you've covered your bases and that it will be enough to avoid accusations of copyright infringement. While giving credit to an author is laudable and you will avoid plagiarism charges by doing so, it does not mean that you won't fall foul of copyright infringement. One exception is work undertaken in an academic environment. Academics extensively footnote their work and this is acceptable practice. But this special exception does not apply in a commercial setting.

### Joint ownership

When you and someone else create a work together, you both own the copyright in the joint work. You are co-owners. Sometimes this might become awkward. Both owners have to agree on virtually all aspects such as modification, extension, and other issues that affect the joint work. In other words, your co-owner in effect has a veto right on all matters.

You may wish to determine whether it is possible at the start of the joint work to purchase the other creator's contribution to avoid long-term problems. For example, if you write a children's storybook, you may consider buying the illustrator's copyright in the drawings. This way, you are the sole owner and can avoid joint ownership issues such as vetoes and stalemate positions.

# CHAPTER 3
# design rights

## WHAT ARE DESIGN RIGHTS?

The **DESIGN** of products has become a **PIVOTAL FACTOR** in today's world. Since the **TECHNICAL EXCELLENCE** and **QUALITY** of competing products are often indistinguishable, **DESIGN** has become

Just think for a moment about the importance of the way things look. The shape of your mobile phone isn't entirely determined by the way it works. It also has a certain design, which might have caused you to buy it instead of another one. Look at your coffee maker. It probably looks different from competitive coffee makers. They all do the same thing, but they look different. Look at the shoes, or slippers, or sandals you are wearing – they probably look different from whatever is on the feet of the next person you see after you read this sentence. Look at your watch – the shape of the watch case, the face of the watch, even the bracelet of your watch might have design features that have nothing to do with the way the watch works. Instead, these are features that help distinguish the way one item looks from another.

a key **SELLING POINT** to customers. No wonder, therefore, that registered **DESIGN FILINGS** have **INCREASED** exponentially. Registered and unregistered design rights cover the appearance or ornamental shape of a product.

In today's marketplace, there are many competing products and everyone wants a piece of the action. New products are flooding into the marketplace from every corner of the globe. Technology is moving in many different directions at the same time. As a result, if you are introducing a new product, you need everything you can think of to distinguish your product from that of your competitor. Certainly having a better product with new and improved features is critical. Patents will protect that. A neat branding campaign will get your product attention. Trade marks will protect that. Good advertising copy and maybe even a theme song for your product are protected by copyright. But all that may not be enough. You want your product to look good, too.

To qualify for unregistered or registered design right protection, your design should have a specific appearance that can be visually recognized.





To get that extra edge, more and more people and companies devote their creative resources to the design of their products or packaging. This is one place where registered and unregistered design rights come into play. Registered and unregistered design rights are also important to many fashion and luxury products. Product design is an integral part of the image of luxury and fashion houses.

If you are a product designer, a package designer, or a company or individual getting ready to launch a new product, you will want to understand what registered and unregistered design rights are, how you obtain them, how they differ from other types of intellectual property protection, and what you can do with your registered and unregistered design rights.

### Examples of design rights

The shape of a new **FERRARI** car, an original design of a **PERFUME BOTTLE**, a new **ORNAMENTAL NECKLACE**, the surface decoration on a **PLATE**, an original shape for a **VASE** or **COFFEE TABLE**, the shape and features of a new **HANDBAG**, the distinctive **PACKAGING** for a product, **BLISTER PACKS** for pills, **COMPUTER-GENERATED SYMBOLS**, graphical user interfaces (**GUI**s), the **MARS** typeface, a **PLASTIC BOTTLE** to contain washing liquid for clothes, the label for a **BOTTLED WATER**, the shape of a **BISCUIT**.

### What can be protected under unregistered or registered design rights?

For example, the distinct features of a new designer handbag, the shape and appearance of a new handle design for cutlery, the distinctive texture applied to an item of jewellery, the distinct aesthetic contours of a perfume bottle, all of which can be visually recognized. To qualify for unregistered or registered design right protection, your design should have a distinctive appearance that can be visually recognized.

Unregistered or registered design rights can protect the ornamental features on any product or other article that can be manufactured. This includes the packaging that is used to sell a product. The protection extends to the shape of an article, three-dimensional designs applied to an article, and, in the case of registered design rights, even two-dimensional ornamental designs applied to an article. The simplest design can have unregistered or registered design right protection. It does not need to be ornate – it just needs to be a feature that does not contribute to the way a product or package works, but instead to the way it looks.

If the new features of your product or package serve a function, you should look to patent law to ascertain whether that functional feature is new and not obvious in relation to what was already out there. But if

**TIP**

**GET IN FIRST**

If someone comes up with the same idea independently, you cannot claim an infringement if you have an unregistered design. So go and apply for a registered design if you can – remember, first in time, first in right!





the feature has an original visual appearance, you are into the realm of designs which can be protected under registered and unregistered design law. Even a simple screwdriver might have certain ornamental features added to give it a nice look.

An unregistered or registered design right will enable you to prevent someone from making, using, or selling your design as depicted in the drawings of your design. Design rights last for a maximum of 15 or 25 years, depending upon whether they are unregistered or registered. Once your unregistered or registered design right expires, the design is there for anyone to make, use, or sell. So get the most out of your design while it lasts.

### Make your unregistered or registered design rights sweat

Yes. This is not a typo. Make them sweat, not make them sweet! Registered and unregistered design rights can work hard for you in an important way. In the chapter on trade marks, I explained that certain product and package designs are not automatically protectable. These designs generally need to be used in a certain way and promoted for a long time before consumers recognize them as brands associated with a single company. So, if you find yourself in that situation, how can you keep others from copying your product or package design while you are trying to build up trade mark rights?

Remember, like diamonds, trade marks can last forever!





Here is where bundling your rights and having a holistic approach to your intellectual property pay off. A registered design right will protect the distinctive features of your product or package design as soon as the certificate issues. Then, while your registered design right is running and protecting the distinctive features of your design, through the use of good advertising campaigns you can teach your consumers that they are not just looking at a pleasant design. They are looking at a product or package design that comes with your brand and is only associated with it.

This bundling of rights or playing off of different types of intellectual property protection can be very useful if you have long-term plans for your designs. But if you are in a field where new styles are coming out each season, concerning yourself with building trade mark rights in your product designs may not be relevant. But don't be surprised if one of your designs becomes a staple and everyone starts associating that product design with your company exclusively. If that happens, and if you promote the design as a brand, you can take advantage of a maximum of the 15 (unregistered) and 25 (registered) years your design right gives you to build up a reputation in your product design as a trade mark. Then, by the time your unregistered or registered design right is ready to retire, you will have trade mark protection. Remember, like diamonds, trade marks can last forever!

### What's inside a registered design?

Unlike patents, registered design rights are very easy to read, or at least at first blush. Information on the designer and any companies he or she has assigned their rights to will be shown along with a drawing, which is usually a three-dimensional-type view of the object that is protected.

As you flip through the pages, you might ask, where is the written description? Where are the claims? Well, in a registered design you are looking at them. There are no written claims in a registered design. The drawings are your claims. A picture is worth a thousand words. And the drawings shown in your registered design should reflect all the design work you have done.

The various drawings or photographs usually have to show your designed article from every angle – not just a three-dimensional view. This means that, when applying to register a design, your drawings or photographs have to line up with one another – every element of your design needs to be consistently shown and clearly depicted. You can't leave anything to the imagination.

After all, the UK government is giving you exclusive rights in your registered design for 25 years, so everyone needs to understand exactly what it is that you claim is your design.

...purely functional features of your design product cannot be protected as a design – it is the visual appearance and aesthetic design features that attract protection.





### What are the basic requirements for registered and unregistered designs?

Just like patents, you cannot get an unregistered or registered design on any old design. Here is where registered and unregistered design rights and patents are the same – to get a registered design, your design or your features need:

▶ To be new or "novel" over everything else that was out there before your design was created.

▶ To have "individual character". Your design or features must be original and not be common-place. But you cannot get a registered or unregistered design for a feature of a product that is solely technical. This is where design rights differ from patents.

**!**

**NOTE OF CAUTION! –** Functional versus visual

Keep in mind that the purely functional features of your design product cannot be protected as a design – it is the visual appearance and aesthetic design features that attract protection. Purely functional and common-place items such as ordinary screws, shoes, bottles, or belts will typically not be protected. However, if you can come up with a zany, eye-catching, highly individualistic screw, which looks quite different from your ordinary garden variety screw, you might have a case.

Your design will obtain unregistered design protection only if it is original and not common-place.



**Novelty** The saying goes that there is nothing new under the sun. However, a registered design will be granted in respect of your design only if it is novel. In other words, your design may not be identical to another design that has already been disclosed to the public elsewhere in the world. This means that your design needs to be new or novel, compared to all information and materials that were out there before your design was complete. Your design will obtain unregistered design protection only if it is original and not common-place. In practice, a design is likely to be original unless copied from another article. It will save you a lot of grief if you establish straight off whether there are prior designs identical to yours. I would therefore suggest you search to determine whether your design is new or not (see www.patent.gov.uk/design/dbase/index.htm).

**LEGAL TEST – Individual character**

The test for individual character relies on the perspective of an informed user who will, in many cases, be the end user of the product. If your design is placed side by side with another, previously disclosed design, and an informed user is able to distinguish between the two, your design fulfils the criteria of individual character.

**UNDERTAKE SEARCHES**

You can undertake searches yourself on the internet, for example, you can use the "**IMAGES**" category of the **GOOGLE** search engine to pull up designs in your field. If your design is the sole of a shoe, type in "shoe soles". Or you can use "jacket design" or "lampshade designs" and so on. This type of search will probably pull up a number of additional designs that are already out there and will help you determine whether your design is likely to be viewed as novel.



**Individual character** To achieve registered design protection, your design should also have "individual character". An example would be if the end user of, say, a new design for a **DUALIT** kettle could distinguish it from a **KENWOOD** kettle already disclosed and on the market.

The saying goes that there is nothing new under the sun. However, a registered design will be granted only if your design is novel. In other words, your design may not be identical to another design that has already been disclosed to the public elsewhere in the world.

Obtaining a good design search before you file will help you look at previous designs to give you an idea of which features of your design have already been protected and which have not. Your intellectual property professional can get the search taken care of and will know how to advise you when you get the results.

### HOW DO I PROVE THAT I AM FIRST IN TIME AND FIRST IN RIGHT?

You should retain good written records of your designs as they are developed. Don't disclose your designs to anyone until you file your application. If you do, assume your design is going to be copied. This means that you should make certain that you are on file with your design right applications before you start showing your designs to others. For unregistered design, as well as physical renditions of the design such as prototypes, do keep a copy in safe custody or a photograph as a record for establishing the date and origin of your design. Remember that first in time is first in right.

Don't disclose your designs to anyone until you file your application. If you do, assume your design is going to be copied. You should be on file with your design right applications before you start showing your designs to others.

**HOW DO I PROVE THAT I AM FIRST IN TIME AND FIRST IN RIGHT?**

It is important to demonstrate unequivocally that you are the owner of the rights in your design. As in the case of proving copyright ownership (see specifically the chapter on copyright, “How do I prove that I am first in time and first in right?”, pp.124–140) you should take certain steps to be in the best position to evidence your ownership:

- Date and sign the original drawing or photocopy of your design.

- Consider having a stamp or seal made with the following wording:

  *I, John Smith, confirm that*
  *I am the designer of this*
  *design, which is an original design*
  *Signed* ____________________
  *Date* ____________________

- Confirm the date of creation with a verification statement by a notary.

- Instead of the stamp and accompanying notary statement, you may wish to sign and swear a statutory declaration (see p.128).

**DEFINITION** – Compulsory licensing

An unregistered design becomes subject to something called "compulsory licensing" in the last five years of its term. This means that anyone will be entitled to a licence to make and sell products by copying the design. The person has to pay you a "compulsory licence fee", though.



## Unregistered design rights

Like copyright, design rights flow automatically upon creation, whether they are registered or not. If you designed it, it is yours – no formalities required. These unregistered design rights last for 10 years after the specific product was first marketed but with a limit of 15 years from the creation of the design.

## Registered design rights

It is highly advisable, though, to register your design at the Design Registry of the UK Patent Office. This registration, which is relatively cheap and easy to obtain, will show and help to clarify proof of your ownership and will give you the right to stop anyone else from using the registered design without your permission (www.patent.gov.uk/design/index.htm). An added bonus is that your registration will last a maximum of 25 years (much longer than unregistered design rights) in the UK.

Your design may also be protected as an unregistered Community design. This is an automatic right that comes into existence once a new design is made available to the public within the European Union. It provides short-term protection (three years) for the shape and configuration of a product.

### Community registered and unregistered designs

If it is likely that your design is going to be used or exploited within the European Union, you should consider filing for a Community registered design. As with a UK registered design, it will assist in proving your ownership of the design and can be relied on to prevent anyone else using the design – not just within the UK but also within the entire European Union. You will have to file a formal application at the Community Designs Office (www.oami.eu.int/en/design/default.htm) but, once granted, registration provides a relatively cheap and easy method of protecting your design and, provided the registration is renewed every five years, will last 25 years.

Some designs come and go from the marketplace so quickly that it will be impossible to obtain a registered design while the article is still for sale. In my view, the best way to deal with this is to get your design applications on file as soon as possible after the design is complete.

Design applications are not nearly as expensive to file as patent applications. If you sit around and wait to determine whether the design is going to have any economic viability, you are losing precious time if it does.

!

**NOTE OF CAUTION! – Design theft**

As soon as your designs are displayed at a trade show, don't be surprised if people take photographs of them or jot down notes, getting ready to copy them. The stealing of designs is so common that some people think there is nothing wrong with it. And there isn't if the creator of the design fails to seek appropriate protection.

Getting a design application on file before you make any display can enable you to tell your competitors and any people looking at the design that it is the subject of protection. You can use "Registered Design Pending" on the actual article, on trade show displays, on advertisements for the product, and on your website. This will let people know that you mean business and that, if they copy your design, they could be in a lot of trouble. One of the beauties of registered designs is that they are not published until they are registered. The first time your competition will see which features you claim are your design is when your design right issues. If you have been smart and careful in the way you claim your design, it will be broad enough to pick up copycats.

The stealing of designs is so common that some people think there is nothing wrong with it.

> **TIP**
>
> **GRACE PERIOD**
>
> Often designers fail to consider the possibility of registering their design prior to disclosing it publicly. Fortunately, in the UK and the EU, there is a 12-month grace period following an initial disclosure of the design. However, if a third party independently comes up with a similar design before you file, that may prevent you from obtaining a valid registration, so it is always wise to register your design as soon as possible.



## FILING A REGISTERED DESIGN APPLICATION

### Make sure your design drawings show your design

You might think that this will be a no-brainer. Unfortunately, even a number of companies that obtain registered design rights and even some professionals think the same thing. They just hand over the designed article to a draftsperson and tell him or her to make a set of drawings showing all the views of the article and then they file. Why not? Isn't this what you are trying to protect, the entire design of the article?

In some cases, it is possible that the entire article has design features all over it that are novel. But in the world of design it is not uncommon to launch a new product that incorporates certain features that have already been out there and others that are new. You might be able to get a registered design on articles with new and old features combined. But why get a registered design that covers old stuff? It only gives your competition an opportunity to make a few changes to the old stuff plus incorporate your new design. Then they will not be infringing your registered design. This is because what you show is what you claim. If you claim a design element that is not critical to your new design and a copycat leaves it off, chances are, they will not be found to have infringed your rights.

TIP

**BE CAREFUL WITH COLOUR PHOTOGRAPHS**

Submitting colour photographs should be done only when a particular colour is a key feature of your design. Remember, if you show that colour as part of your design, your competitor can probably avoid infringement by copying the shape of the design but depicting it in a different colour. I discourage using photographs at all; and you should forget using colour photographs unless colour is an actual feature of your design.

So, just like anything else in the world of intellectual property, you have to think about what it is about your design that is new and novel. That is what you want to protect. Then communicate that to your intellectual property professional so that he or she understands and then can go about protecting just that feature in the application. For example, if you are trying to protect the design of a new perfume bottle, but there is nothing new about the cap, then why include the cap in your design?

### Registering individual features

How do you go about protecting certain features? If you were to submit drawings showings bits and pieces of an article, the Examiner or a court would not understand what the article was and would refuse your application on that basis. As a result, the Patent Office has come up with detailed rules that define exactly how you can depict your product and package designs when you are filing a design right application. For example, you can use dotted lines to show portions of an article that are not part of your claimed design. This way, the Examiner will understand the overall article your design is used on but he or she will also understand the feature of it that you claim as your design.

Design cuts across almost everything in the marketplace, so the ins and outs and nuances of what to show and how to show it for each category of articles will vary.

Your intellectual property professional and the draftsperson you use should be familiar with these rules. The Patent Office will also accept black and white photographs of all views of the design you would like to claim if you mount the photographs on paper. But, unless every feature of your product is new, this is not the way to go. It sounds easy, but you get what you pay for.

**NOTE OF CAUTION! –** Be very specific

The Patent Office is very literal with the "drawings" you submit. If you use a photograph, you are claiming everything in the picture as your design. Even if you are cool with that, you still have to watch your step. If the photograph shows your designed object sitting on a table, and you do not tell the Examiner that the table is not part of the claimed design, he or she will assume it is. The same applies to reflections in the photograph, trade marks that might be displayed on the product, and all other elements depicted in the photograph.

Registered design applications are not examined in the way that patents are; the formalities are checked but there is no difficult examination. They are sometimes registered as quickly as six to eight weeks after they are filed if all legal requirements are met, but the process can take three to four months.

Once your registered design right has issued, you have the exclusive right to make use of and sell the features depicted in the drawings in your registered design.



**Office Actions and registration**

The most common questions that will arise will relate to your drawings, since these are essentially all that your design application comprises. Be nice to your Examiners and read the tips on dealing with intellectual property professionals, pp.243–246.

Once everything is in order, you will receive a Certificate of Registration. At this juncture treat yourself to a piña colada or other cocktail of your choice to celebrate, but remember to pay your renewal fees on time.

When your registered design right issues, you now have the exclusive right to make use of and sell the features depicted in the drawings in your registered design. This will last 25 years from the date the registration issues. You do need to pay renewal fees every five years, but you do not need to use the design during this period.

Of course, if you are trying to develop trade mark rights, you should be using it – and using it a lot. But one other advantage of a registered design is that even after you stop making the article with this design and perhaps move on to other designs, if someone rips off that earlier design, you can still take action. A competitor cannot attack your registered design because you have not used it.

**TIP**

**YOU DO NOT HAVE TO SUE EVERY INFRINGER**

Bear in mind that there is no obligation for you to sue every infringer. Unlike trade mark enforcement, you can pick and choose at random which infringers you wish to sue. Since litigation is expensive, you may prefer to go after the big guys and leave the small ones alone.





## IF MY DESIGN IS COPIED WITHOUT MY CONSENT BY SOMEONE ELSE, WHAT CAN I DO?

The standard for infringement of an unregistered design is whether there has been an exact or substantial copy of the design. For a registered design, there is no need to prove your registered design has been copied. The standard for infringement of a registered design is if the alleged infringing design creates the same overall impression on the informed user. Once again, there is no magical litmus test to determine whether such an infringement has taken place. It is advisable to consult an intellectual property lawyer on this point.

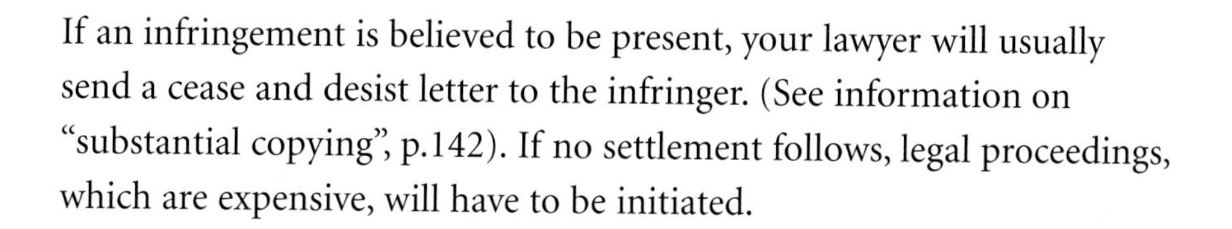

If an infringement is believed to be present, your lawyer will usually send a cease and desist letter to the infringer. (See information on "substantial copying", p.142). If no settlement follows, legal proceedings, which are expensive, will have to be initiated.

**LEGAL TEST** – The test for infringement

The standard that the courts use in determining whether or not a registered or unregistered design is infringed is essentially whether the defendant's design is substantially the same as the claimed design. The focus is on deception of the ordinary observer, where one design is confused with the other.

As I already warned, and as you may already know from experience, people will copy your design the moment they see it. If that happens to you, and you have a registered design application on file, you should consider sending a warning letter. You do not need to say when you expect your design right to issue. If the other person knows, he or she might try to dump as much product on the marketplace as possible before your registered design issues. If you say nothing, and keep in mind that the opposition cannot figure it out, since your registered design application is confidential and is not published, he or she will move forward at his or her own peril.

**NOTE OF CAUTION! –** Unjustified threats

Care must be taken in drafting such a letter if you have unregistered or registered design rights, because if you are considered to have made unjustified threats, you may face stiff penalties. You should therefore get your intellectual property professional to advise and draft a suitable letter.

If your competitor does not stop, remember, you cannot sue someone for registered design right infringement until your registered design right issues. However, you may have a claim for unregistered design right infringement. You should therefore sit down with your lawyer and be comfortable that your competitor's article incorporates your claimed design or any unregistered rights you may have. Here is where having

If you and your lawyer believe that a copied device infringes your registered or unregistered design, a strong letter should be sent demanding that all sales of the copied design be discontinued. You can also ask for money based on any manufacture, sale, or use of the articles made with your claimed design.

Nothing prevents you from claiming both copyright and unregistered or registered design rights in your creation...





been very careful with what you show in your drawings and what you don't show as your claimed design will be essential. If your competitor has added something to the article to make it look different, that does not mean that your design is not infringed. He or she still copied what you claimed. In fact, your design may have been improved. But that does not mean that your competitor is allowed to copy what you have protected. But if your claimed design has features that are shown, which your competitor has not used, you are probably out of luck.

If you and your lawyer believe that the copied device infringes your unregistered or registered design, a strong letter should be sent demanding that all sales of the copied design be discontinued. You can also ask for money based on any manufacture, sale, or use of the articles made with your claimed design. And if you have been successfully selling your product at this stage, you may also be able to claim that you have trade mark rights in it. This is where approaching your intellectual property holistically is essential. Think through all the elements that your competitor may have infringed. Does the design incorporate any trade marks, logos, design, or even product design that has taken on trade mark significance? Are there patterns or other visual elements that might be protected under copyright law? Is there a way that the article works that you have protected or are in the process of protecting under patents? Is this a competitor who has found out critical information about trade secrets by hiring a former employee? If you have a reasonable opponent, he or she will realize an error has been made. A letter might come back with some obnoxious statements, taking some pot shots at your rights. But if it says anything that indicates a willingness to settle, in my view it is better to settle than litigate. But, if you do end up in court, you will have earned brownie points with the judge if you can establish that you attempted to settle the matter first.

## TIPS AND TRAPS

### Ownership

Be aware that, if you commission someone to create a design, you will be the first owner of the unregistered or registered design right in it, unlike the position in relation to commissioning a copyright work, where the person who created the work will own the copyright.

### Bundling

Nothing prevents you from claiming both copyright and unregistered or registered design rights in your creation, provided it fulfils the qualifications of all rights. It is quite helpful to bundle your rights in this fashion since your scope of protection will increase. (See the section on bundling your intellectual property, pp.238–242.)

# CHAPTER 4
# trade secrets

## WHAT ARE TRADE SECRETS?

Trade secrets cover **CONFIDENTIAL** business information including **TECHNOLOGICAL KNOW-HOW**, **FORMULAS**, **PROCESSES**, **COMPUTER CODES**, **DEVICES**, and similar information that is kept confidential to provide a competitive edge in the market-place. The next time you walk into **HARRODS**, close your eyes and breathe in. Unless you have a bad cold, you will sense a combination of **NATURAL** and **SYNTHETIC FRAGRANCES**

If you are a cook, a pastry chef, a winegrower, an organic farmer, a chocolate maker, a perfume designer, a computer programmer, or if you are in a host of other businesses that rely on secret recipes, formulas, computer code, and techniques to help differentiate your products and

that can range in price from a few pounds for a bottle to thousands of pounds for an ounce. Next, stop by **LA MAISON DU CHOCOLAT** and sample some of the fantastic chocolate creations available there. After that, try a **REALLY EXPENSIVE GLASS OF WINE** and see whether it is any different from the **JUGS OF WINE** you have shared with friends. Now that you smell great and have enjoyed some fabulous dessert and drink, it's time to read this chapter.

concoctions from those of others, you will appreciate how much work it takes to learn just the basics. And then there are the secrets that you finally devise that separate your creations from everything else out there. These secrets are valuable business assets and you will know when you have one.

Trade secrets conjure up images of cloak-and-dagger secrecy and it is true that, typically, only a few privileged individuals will have knowledge of a particular trade secret.





But it is not just recipes, computer code, formulas, and techniques for foods, desserts, wines, and fragrances that you might want to keep secret. Regardless of the type of business you are in, you no doubt have a list of customers or clients who are loyal and you know exactly what they need. You have a list of suppliers and other vendors who you have come to rely on to get things done through a lot of trial and error. These people and businesses help your own business run efficiently. And if you need to get your product manufactured, you know there are lots of kinks to iron out, not just to get the product made but to get it out the door and onto shelves. This sort of know-how can make the difference between making it and breaking it, regardless of how good your products and services are.

Secret recipes, formulas, computer code, and techniques, as well as confidential business information and know-how that can be used to help your business, help you manufacture product, and help you get it to market effectively and efficiently, fall into the category of trade secrets, as long as they are not readily available by reading books, consulting experts, or buying off-the-shelf computer programs. This information is very valuable – it took a lot of time and effort to develop, it is your own private information, and it is a real asset to your business. Without it your product could lose its competitive edge.

Trade secrets conjure up images of cloak-and-dagger secrecy and it is true that, typically, only a few privileged individuals will have knowledge of any particular trade secret. The famous **COCA-COLA** trade secret, **MERCHANDISE 7X**, is said to be known to only a few people at the **COCA-COLA** Company in Atlanta. Disclosure of such a valuable trade secret to anyone else would amount to a breach of confidence.

Confidentiality, therefore, lies at the heart of trade secret protection. If the information is disclosed, or is in the public domain, it is not confidential and no trade secret protection can be provided.

Trade secret protection does not share some of the preconditions of patent or copyright protection. For instance, to qualify for trade secret protection the information does not have to be either "novel" or "be expressed in a tangible medium of expression". Prime candidates for trade secret protection are information or ideas that cannot easily or accurately be reverse engineered.

Trade secrets can clearly be very valuable and their misappropriation can be extremely serious. For example, in a case involving several former employees of a chip-design software maker, who left the company and formed a competitor, there was evidence that they took some of the software maker's most valuable source code with them – an outright theft. The violations were so severe that criminal charges were brought. In addition, hundreds of millions of pounds had to be paid. It is interesting to note that employee theft usually not only involves trade secret infringement but often copyright infringement too!

Trade secret is the vehicle often used to protect valuable new technology. The protection may last for only a limited period of time (i.e. before patent applications for that technology are filed and published), or it may last indefinitely when there is no commercial reason for the trade secret ever to be disclosed.

### Examples of trade secrets

**COCA-COLA**'s **MERCHANDISE 7X** – the formula for the best-selling fizzy drink – is the poster boy of trade secrets. The complexities of a **PERFUME FORMULA** may also merit trade secret protection. Trade secrets also exist as a form of protection for some **COMPUTER PROGRAMS**, ideas for **NEW PRODUCTS**, **TECHNOLOGICAL KNOW-HOW** of business systems, an idea for a **TELEVISION SERIES**, **CUSTOMER AND SUPPLIER LISTS** belonging to a business, a **METHOD OF MANUFACTURE**, financial information such as **SALES FIGURES**, **MARKETING PLANS** and **STRATEGIES**, **SURVEY METHODS** used by professional pollsters, a **CHEMICAL FORMULA** for a brand new product such as perfume, and **INGREDIENTS** and **COMBINATIONS** for new recipes.

Trade secrets aren't registered, since they are by definition your own secret materials.





## HOW DO I PROVE THAT I AM ENTITLED TO TRADE SECRET PROTECTION?

Trade secrets aren't registered, since they are by definition your own secret materials. So, if you get into a dispute with someone who steals one, you will have to be able to prove what you had at a given time and that you kept it secret. The following sections give you some pointers on how to do that.

### Keep it secret

You must be able to show that you are keeping your trade secret confidential. To prove this point convincingly, keep records of the steps you have taken to ensure the physical protection of your trade secret. For instance, is the formula of your trade secret kept in a vault for safe keeping? What kind of access is there to your trade secret? Having a detailed business policy for handling your trade secrets is a good start. This applies to chefs too!

If you get into a dispute with someone who steals a trade secret, you will have to be able to prove what you had at a given time and that you kept it secret.

**TIP**

**THINK ABOUT PATENT AND COPYRIGHT PROTECTION TOO**

As trade secret protection and patent or copyright protection often overlap, you should seriously consider following the steps outlined in the "How do I show that I am first in time and first in right?" sections under copyright, pp.124–140 and under patents, pp.208–213.





Always remember that access to the information should be highly restricted. When information is shared, make sure that all correspondence is at all times clearly marked as "Confidential". Don't leave confidential materials or apparatus out in the open. Don't give tours of your manufacturing facilities or other areas where outsiders could have access to your trade secrets, unless they have signed "nondisclosure agreements".

Don't even give your own employees access to your trade secrets unless they need them to perform their tasks. And keep written records of who visits, when they visit, and the purpose of their visit. Larger companies make all visitors wear badges so everyone knows who is a visitor. Whatever you do, if trade secrets are involved in your business, you should control the whereabouts of people on your premises to show that you have a policy of keeping your information secret.

Remember: the smaller the circle of people who are in the know, the better – not only for commercial security, but also for legal reasons.

Remember: "an ounce of prevention is worth a pound of cure".





## Confidentiality letters

You must be able to show that, whenever you have disclosed your trade secret to someone else, it has been under obligation of confidence. By far the best way to prove this point is to request that everyone to whom you disclose your trade secret signs a "confidentiality letter" or "nondisclosure agreement" (NDA). No wonder the digirati have been handing out one-page NDAs like business cards during commercial gatherings ever since the dotcom revolution. For an example of a typical NDA see Appendix 6, pp.272–273. Remember: the smaller the circle of people who are in the know, the better – not only for commercial security, but also for legal reasons. Even a chef's assistant should sign an NDA – don't be shy, it's your creation that's at stake.

!

**NOTE OF CAUTION!** – Reluctance to sign NDAs

From bitter experience I have to warn you that you will often encounter resistance from big corporations. They may not be willing to sign an NDA when you approach them with a proposal for commercial cooperation. Their reason, sometimes justifiably so, is that they may be working on a similar project. What I have done in these circumstances is to disclose the end result of the trade secret without revealing the confidential know-how. This should work most of the time, but sometimes it is impossible to reveal the end result without giving away the trade secret itself.

In cases where you are talking to a corporate gorilla, you will either have to assume the risk of disclosure in order to profit from a possible business opportunity or you could consider filing a patent where feasible. You may also want to give thought to slapping a copyright notice on your original written materials before handing them over. Copyright is not the ideal vehicle for protecting confidential information, but the notice may have a deterrent effect. Remember: "an ounce of prevention is worth a pound of cure".

### Keep good records

You should keep good written records of what you have at each stage. Since there is no official filing, your records and how they are kept will help establish what information you had at any given time. And keep them in a safe place where only the most trusted people, who have signed confidentiality agreements, have access to them.

## WHEN DOES SOMEONE INFRINGE MY TRADE SECRET?

If someone who is under an obligation of confidence discloses your trade secret, it is an infringement, in the same way that someone who breaks into your space violates your rights. But proving what you had and showing you keep it secret can be a tough job. You should consult an intellectual property lawyer at this juncture who will advise you on litigation.

If your particular trade secret is new, novel, and nonobvious, you should consider whether it would be advantageous to protect it as a patent.





**TIPS AND TRAPS**

**Trade secret or patent?**

If your particular trade secret is new, novel, and nonobvious, you should consider whether it would be advantageous to protect it as a patent.

If your secret could be reverse engineered, you should seriously contemplate filing a patent application to guard against a competitor pre-empting you by approaching the Patent Office first – whether such a competitor developed the same invention through independent research or not. A pre-emption may allow your competitors to exclude you from the market.

**DEFINITION** – Reverse engineering

Reverse engineering is when your competitors are able to figure out, through careful analysis, the different unique components that make up your product or service, their composition, and their relative quantity.

However, if your invention is not capable of being reverse engineered, it may be the case that trade secret protection will offer the better route. You may very well gain a competitive advantage by protecting your invention as a trade secret.

As a trade secret your invention is not limited to the patent term of 20 years and may continue for as long as it is kept confidential. For example, **COCA-COLA**'s secret formula is now over 100 years old and is still going strong. An added bonus is that the invention does not have to be disclosed to the public as part of a patent application. This should protect you against imitators and infringers.

A trade secret may continue for as long as it is kept confidential. **COCA-COLA**'s secret formula is now over 100 years old and is still going strong.

Finally, the long-term cost involved with trade secret protection is often substantially less than obtaining and maintaining a patent.

A careful strategy may provide you with substantially more layers of protection than if you relied on one set of rights only.



**HOW CAN I BUNDLE MY ASSETS?**

You may wish to consider bundling your various rights. A careful strategy may provide you with substantially more layers of protection than if you relied on one set of rights alone.

For instance, you may wish to preserve part of your invention for trade secret protection, insofar as it cannot be reverse engineered. The remainder of the invention, which can be reverse engineered, could possibly be filed as a patent. Furthermore, some aspects may also qualify for copyright protection.

Always consider all possible scenarios in order to secure maximum coverage for protection purposes. For example, certain computer programs may qualify not only for trade secret protection but also for patent and copyright protection.

Do keep in mind that if you file a patent application or a copyright submission to the US Copyright Office, you will need to disclose your invention. It is useful to know, however, that when seeking protection for computer programs you do not have to submit an entire copy of your source code, but only have to provide sufficient material to identify your computer program.

# CHAPTER 5
# patents

## WHAT IS A PATENT?

When you turn off the **LAMP** at night and your head hits the **PILLOW**, the last thing running through your mind (at least I hope) is whether your **PILLOW** has any patented features. The same

The truth is, wherever you are sitting as you read this paragraph, if you look around you, it is likely that within a few feet are several items that are patented or are made under a patented process. This includes, for example, the chair you are sitting on and the method of weaving the carpeting underneath you. And if you are lucky enough to be on the beach reading this, there is probably a patent on your beach chair, or on the material your beach umbrella is made of, or on the suntan lotion you just put on. And if you are at your desk, there are patents covering your computer hardware and software. And your telephone – both the satellite system and land lines, as well as all the equipment, are or have been patented.

goes for the **MATTRESS** – what about patents on that? Who invented the **PILL** you just took? What kinds of patents are protecting the **LAMP** on your nightstand? And hey, don't forget the **LIGHT BULB**!

You don't need a laboratory where everyone runs around in white coats speaking in hushed tones for inventions to be created. People who work in such locations may very well create great inventions. But it is just as likely that your best friend's mother, or the person sitting next to you when you go to renew your driver's licence, and yes, even you, have as much of an opportunity to invent something as anyone else. Will your invention change the course of humankind? If it does, be sure to tell everyone that you read this book. But your invention can be just as worthy of patent protection if it is a new innovation and is useful to others, as long as it is not obvious compared to everything that is already out there.

Anyone who has an original idea and takes the time and effort to develop it into something usable can be an inventor.



The people who conceive inventions are all influenced by everything that comes before them. They are smart enough, reasonable enough, and motivated enough to take the time and effort to recognize a new idea. But we can all come up with an idea or a dream. Invention is about turning these dreams and ideas into actual working things or processes. This is what separates inventors from the rest of the creative pack. Inventors are skilled enough and talented enough to build something or develop a process with their dreams and ideas.

It is not just earth-moving innovations that can be protected under the patent laws. There is always room for improvement. You can improve on existing things and build on them, making them better, easier, cheaper, or more efficient to use. You can also expand on basic inventions. After all, the light bulb is great, but laser light technology has brought about both incredible medical advances and also lots of entertaining light shows.

Anyone who has an original idea and takes the time and effort to develop it into something usable can be an inventor. So can people who improve on these foundations. If you are one of them, you need to know how to protect your inventions, how to reap the rewards, and how you can build on these to get a better product or process into the marketplace. It is not just genius but perseverance that counts.

**DEFINITION** – Patents

A patent essentially protects an invention, typically new or improved products or processes in the field of science and technology. Patent protection generally covers functional or technical features of these products and processes.

The rights that flow from a patent can be very useful to an entrepreneur. A patent gives an inventor the exclusive right to manufacture, use, or sell his or her invention free of competition in the countries where the patent is granted. In other words, he or she has the right to stop others from doing so. In the UK this exclusivity lasts for 20 years from the date of the patent application.

Patents can cover any technology or field, but they are generally characterized as electrical, biotechnology, software, chemical, and mechanical. Patents cover literally hundreds of thousands of products that you see in stores or in day-to-day business, ranging from vitamin pills to flat-screen televisions, to the windscreen wiper on your car. They also cover satellite systems, methods for downloading music, and endless types of plastics. Artificial implants or organs? Patented. And the methods for implanting them? Patented. You get the idea.

Patents cannot be renewed after 20 years.





### Examples of patents

The telephone, the light bulb, **AMAZON'S ONE-CLICK CHECKOUT** system, **VIAGRA** pills, **WINDOWS** software, the **DYSON** vacuum cleaner, a windsurf board and rigging, **MECCANO** toys, the ballpoint pen, the artificial heart, **CATSEYES** road reflectors, the computer mouse, and the cut of a diamond are all examples of past or current patents. Electronic devices and computer software are widely covered by patents. For example, the latest version of the freely available **ADOBE ACROBAT READER** program is covered by no less than 40 patents, while the company **ALTAVISTA** owns more than 50 search engine patents. Indeed, the US Supreme Court has stated that "everything under the sun that is made by man" is technically patentable. Keep in mind, though, that UK law is not quite so expansive.

### What do patents protect?

Patents can protect a basic product and the way it is made, as well as the specific features of that product or process. With your patent you can exclude anyone else from making, using, or selling your invention. Most patents last for 20 years from the filing date. But there are maintenance fees to pay along the way. Patents cannot be renewed after 20 years.

Remember that there are maintenance fees to pay along the way for your patent.

**ADD VALUE**

The value of a patent extends well beyond its term. You should therefore develop a trade mark for your invention. Then you can protect your product and charge royalties for the use of your trade mark after the expiration of the patent term on the basis of your trade mark rights.

**NOTE OF CAUTION!** – Patents expire!

Once your patent expires, your invention is there for anyone to make, use, or sell. So you want to get the most out of your patent while it is alive. Before filing, keep in mind that you may wish to preserve part of your invention for trade secret protection insofar as it cannot be reverse engineered. The remainder of the invention that can be reverse engineered could then be filed as a patent.

It is not at all uncommon for a company to own many patents that cover what you might think of as a single product. Patents also cover improvements made to patented products and processes; that way companies can have a series of patents that extend over a long period of time. Consumers benefit from these improvements. And so do the patent owners, since the fruits of their development activities on existing products and processes lead to new patent protection. Some people call this built-in obsolescence. I call it development and progress.

If done properly, a patent will prevent your competition from making, using, or selling whatever is claimed in your patent. It gives you a competitive edge so that you can develop a group of loyal customers who will want your product even after the patent expires. And if the demand for your patented product is greater than you can handle, you can license it out and get royalties.

## What's inside a patent?

**Abstract** When you first see a patent it can be off-putting (you can see an example at www.fromedisontoipod.com). They often have a technical drawing and a description of the invention on the cover. This is called the "abstract". But don't judge a patent by its cover. You have to open it and start reading to really understand what is covered. A patent has several sections, and can vary in length, depending on the nature of the invention being protected.

**Drawings** Patents are generally accompanied by detailed drawings that clearly and accurately show all aspects of the invention. A good background to the area of the invention is provided so that you can understand how this invention fits into the real world. And an explanation is provided as to why and what the inventor has come up with and how this invention is new and sufficiently different from everything else that is out there.

Don't judge a patent by its cover. You have to open it and start reading to really understand what is covered.

...it is everything as a whole in your patent that will define your invention and give meaning to what you claim.



**Written description** The drawings are then followed by a detailed description, which explains the various elements in the drawings and how they work together.

**Claims** At the end of all this is a series of numbered paragraphs that carefully and consistently define exactly what your invention is. These are known as the "claims" and provide the legal definition of your invention. They stake out the land that your invention covers.

Claims can be difficult to read as they are very detailed. But, like Shakespeare, after a few minutes of reading claims, you can start to follow them. They should make a lot of sense, even if they are technical. But it is everything as a whole in your patent that will define your invention and give meaning to what you claim. It is in a patent specification where your hard labours, no matter how simple or complex they may be, are defined and where you stake out your territory.

### What do patents cover?

You cannot get a patent on any old thing. But show me a new thing and I bet there is an invention involved – maybe even several inventions. Just make certain that it is:

- New.
- Inventive.
- Has industrial application.

Given these criteria, some ideas are generally known to be nonpatentable. In the UK, such ideas include:

- Scientific or mathematical discoveries or theories.
- A method or scheme for doing business.
- Literary, artistic, or musical works (however, these works can be protected by copyright).

**DEFINITION** – Business method patents

Business method patents cover methods for doing business, for example **AMAZON'S ONE-CLICK CHECKOUT**. Business method patent is a term used in the US since the dotcom era, and is one of the key areas where US law is more liberal than UK law in terms of what may be protected by way of patent. The US has significantly opened the door in relation to business methods to provide protection to a much broader range of inventions in the digital era. In some cases, the range of protection has become so extreme that critics have referred to this as the "silliness standard", for example a patent for "a method of making tests, assessments, surveys, and lesson plans with images and sound files and posting online" or a method of training cleaners using only pictorial displays. The UK and Europe have not shown the same willingness to extend their fields of patentable inventions along similar lines.

You cannot get a patent on any old thing. But show me a new thing and I bet there is an invention involved.

## HOW DO I ENSURE THAT I AM FIRST IN TIME AND FIRST IN RIGHT?

There is one simple answer to this question: make your way to the Patent Office as soon as you possibly can. Patents are time critical, so stake your claim first before your competitors beat you to the prize. Provided your invention is not more suited to claiming protection as a trade secret or another form of intellectual property (more fully discussed above in the chapter on trade secrets, pp.182–193), you should attempt to file your patent application at the UK Patent Office as soon as is practically possible.

**DEFINTION** – Provisional patent applications

In time-critical situations you can always file what is called a provisional patent application to obtain a filing date quickly. A provisional (i.e. unfinished) application includes a description of the invention but need not have any claims. Within a year of filing a provisional application, a more complete application with a full set of claims should be filed.

The official filing date of your patent is pivotal, since it constitutes the priority date if you wish to extend your patent internationally. The filing date in each country also starts the commencement of your 20-year patent term in that country.

We have all come up with an idea that we think about "patenting". But, as you know by now, you can't patent an idea. You have to get the good ideas out of your head and into a working prototype or description. This requires a lot of sweat and time. It separates the dreamers from the inventors!

### Make sure it's yours

You should ensure that your patents belong to you. If you are the one who conceived the invention as set out in the claims of the patent application, then you are the inventor in the eyes of the law.

**Independent inventors** In the sense of the genius inventor working in a lonely garret, independent inventors have become a rarity. Often invention is a joint endeavour or there are contributions from other experts that assist the lead inventor in development.

We have all come up with an idea that we think about patenting. But, as you know by now, you can't patent an idea. You have to get the ideas out of your head and into a working prototype or description. This requires a lot of sweat and time. It separates the dreamers from the inventors! It is not uncommon for two people working together to contribute to what ends up being one claimed invention. This can happen among friends. Or it can happen in a research and development environment, where people are working together to accomplish common goals.

If you conceived the invention as set out in the patent application, then you are the inventor in the eyes of the law.

TIP

**CONSOLIDATE YOUR OWNERSHIP RIGHTS**

In situations where there is a joint endeavour it is crucial that you consolidate your ownership rights. Get the number of true inventors correct. You have to name each inventor who has been involved in the development process and who contributed to the invention. If you miss a name, the validity of your patent could be jeopardized. So do ensure that the right people are named as inventors in the patent application.

**NOTE OF CAUTION! –** Ownership

Whether your invention was created by you in your garage, on a napkin over lunch with a friend, or in a sealed laboratory where everyone wears white coats and hairnets, you must get the name or the names of the inventors correct when you file your application. Don't insist on naming yourself as an inventor because of pride, ego, or improved job opportunities. And don't let anyone else leave you out if you are the true inventor or one of the inventors. If the wrong names are provided, or if an incomplete list of inventors is identified in the patent application, the entire patent could be jeopardized.

Besides, the last thing you want is for people to come out of the woodwork after the invention becomes a commercial success. Where possible, you should have minor contributors or subcontractors agree to assign their rights in the invention to you. Ask your patent lawyer to help you with this. Such a move will help you consolidate your ownership in the patent – as far as possible all rights in the invention should belong to you.

Prior art notably includes other patents that predate yours, not only in the UK but elsewhere in the world.

**DEBUNKING THE MYTH –** Inventorship is not the same as ownership

Just because someone is an inventor does not mean that he or she has to share in the fruits of the patent. Inventorship is not the same as ownership. This can be taken care of using agreements where people assign all their rights to you or your company. But getting an assignment from an inventor or co-inventor does not mean that he or she is not an inventor. It simply means that he or she is giving up all rights in the invention to you or your company. Your patent professional can walk you through this. You would think that this would be simple. But ego, jealousy, and competitive spirit can get in the way of this process. Make sure you do not let it happen to your invention, or everything you have worked for could be lost.

### A thorny issue: the rights of employer versus employee

It is important to keep in mind that, if you have developed an invention as an employee within the scope of your employment, the invention will usually belong to your employer. This may be the case even if you have made the invention in your own free time. This is an issue that often gives rise to great bitterness and misunderstanding. You should consult your patent professional on this essential point.

If you work in a corporate environment, or are a subcontractor or consultant, when you are hired you will probably be asked to sign an agreement stating that any inventions you create or contribute to

> **TIP**
> **CLARIFY YOUR POSITION**
> Read agreements with employers carefully. You should make sure that any inventions that have nothing to do with your job and that are created outside work can still be owned by you. And if you are a consultant working with a number of different clients, you should make sure that the scope of your task has been carefully defined in the contract. You don't want to end up in a situation where two clients are telling you that you are obliged to assign the same invention to each of them.

will belong to your employer or the company hiring you. You should definitely have a lawyer look at all these agreements so that you fully understand what you are giving up.

Remember that if you have developed an invention as an employee within the scope of your employment, the invention will usually belong to your employer. This may be the case even if you have made the invention in your own free time.

If you are pretty good at what you do, you might be able to negotiate an agreement where you get to have a piece of the action from any patents that issue. In some cases, where your invention is a zinger, the law helps you. If you are an employee and you have made an invention that has been patented by your employer, you may have a right to claim a "fair share" (like an additional bonus) if it is decided by the court that the patent has been of "outstanding benefit" to your employer.

Your invention must embody a creative idea that has a notable difference from all other instances of prior art.



## HOW DO I QUALIFY FOR PATENT PROTECTION?

### New or novel

Your invention must be new or novel to qualify for patent protection. In other words, your invention must be new compared to all the information that is available to the public before the date of your patent application.

**DEFINITION** – Prior art

Any information that was disclosed to the public and predates your invention is referred to as "prior art". Prior art includes other people's stuff, as well as some of your own. Prior art based on other people's stuff includes publications that were available anywhere in the world. If this prior disclosure includes everything you claim as your invention, you are out of luck. You cannot claim that invention in a patent. Prior art also includes patents published before the date of your invention not only in the UK but elsewhere in the world. Thus, your invention cannot be preceded by another invention anywhere else. This is where patent searches become highly relevant. And it's not just the claims of prior patents that are considered prior art, it's everything the patent shows or describes.

The requirement to be new compared to all prior art sounds daunting, but the novelty test is not impregnable. Your patent can be denied only if one reference discloses each and every feature of your invention.

### Inventiveness

Your invention must not be an obvious modification of what is already known by referring to prior art. Your invention must embody a creative idea that has a notable difference from all other instances of prior art. This is often an important hurdle to overcome with Examiners at the Patent Office when applying for a patent.

You will have to convince the Examiner that your claimed invention involves some kind of technical innovation or other creative idea that has a notable difference from what is cited. You can often tweak the wording of your claims. In doing so, you are cutting back on what you stake out, so do it carefully.

Unfortunately, this tends to be a grey area because there is no bright line standard for what is obvious and not inventive. In fact, the yardstick according to patent law is whether or not the invention is obvious to a person skilled in the relevant field. Defining this fictional person can be a tad elusive. Nonetheless, I do know that this fictional person is neither the best expert in the field nor your weekend tinkerer but someone with an average level of skill in the relevant field. This may help your assessment on whether you believe your creation meets the inventiveness requirement.

Your inventions are not protected until a patent issues.





**Industrial application**

Your invention may also be capable of industrial application. In other words, your invention can be made or used in some kind of industry. This requirement generally does not create a problem.

Do note that a prototype of your invention does not have to be built. You should, however, be confident that your invention will work in the way described in your patent application.

Unlike trade marks, where you can rely on unregistered common law rights, and copyright that exists from the moment of creation, your inventions are not protected until a patent issues.

**GET PROFESSIONAL HELP**

**TIP**

In the UK, you do not need a lawyer to file a patent application. You can file on your own. But you can also give yourself open heart surgery. Don't do it. A patent professional who is registered to practise before the UK Patent Office can file your patent application. Some patent solicitors also draft and file patent applications for their clients.



## WHAT SHOULD I DO TO PROTECT MY INVENTION?

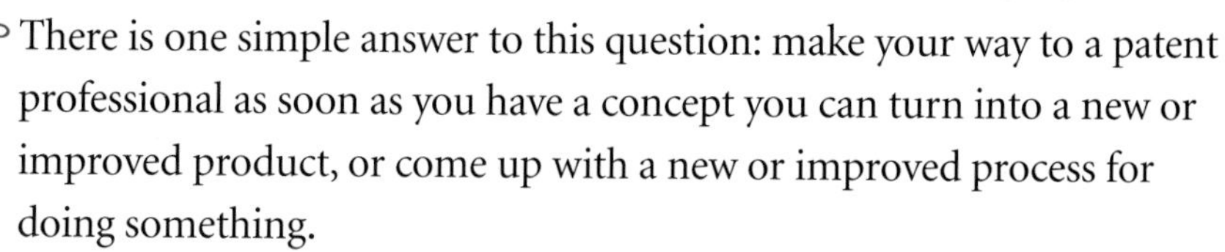

There is one simple answer to this question: make your way to a patent professional as soon as you have a concept you can turn into a new or improved product, or come up with a new or improved process for doing something.

Unlike trade marks, where you can rely on unregistered common law rights, and copyright that exists from the moment of creation, your inventions are not protected until a patent issues. Because of this, many inventors are still figuring out exactly what their invention is when they go to their patent professional. If your patent professional thinks you have something you can protect, make sure he or she files a patent application in the Patent Office as soon as possible.

**!**

**NOTE OF CAUTION!** – Time is ticking

It is vital to understand that your own activities in relation to your invention can cause you to lose the ability to patent it. In fact, publicly disclosing your invention in any manner before applying for a patent is equivalent to dropping a 10-ton weight on your potential patent rights. Your potential patent will be crushed to smithereens if a patent application covering your invention was not filed beforehand. Don't let that happen to your inventions. Let your patent professional know if you plan to disclose your invention so he or she knows that the clock with 10-ton weight is ticking and when it will go off. Remember, you can be your invention's worst enemy.

If you have not filed a patent application covering your invention before you disclose it, it gets crushed to smithereens.



Selecting a good patent solicitor or attorney to persuade the Examiner of the merits of your application is a big plus and can significantly ease your way through the application process. I will refer to the solicitor or attorney here as your "patent professional". You can visit http://www.cipa.org.uk for your choice of patent professionals.

The official filing date of your patent is also a key to getting protection around the world. If you file your foreign applications within one year after your first application is on file, you can extend it internationally (see pp.248–250 more information on filing abroad).

The sooner you file, the better. If you are in a field where developments are coming fast and furious, your delay could let other people file before you and their patents might be cited against you.

Be aware, be very aware: it is laughably easy to "disclose" your invention.

!

**NOTE OF CAUTION! –** Don't disclose your invention!

I already told you about this. But some things deserve a repeat performance and this is one of them. And I've added a twist of lime in case you're getting bored. This rule sounds obvious and easy to comply with. But it's not. If you are a creative type, you are probably pretty enthused about what you come up with. However, if I had collected a tenner for every inventor who has cornered me at a cocktail party asking for patent advice and in the process inadvertently disclosed the details of the invention, I would be retired and living on a tropical island by now. Be aware, be very aware: it is laughably easy to "disclose" your invention.

A few examples

By talking to acquaintances at a meeting or cocktail party (I told you I'd add some lime), by publishing a short discussion of your invention on your website, a chat room, or in a not widely circulated technical newsletter, by giving a lecture at an academic conference, or by describing your invention to a potential customer, you will have fallen foul of the nondisclosure requirement. In other words, if you reveal your invention verbally, demonstrate its virtues, advertise your invention, or publish an article on it before you apply for a patent, you are making your invention public or disclosing it. And then it's too late to patent it.

Discussions with your patent professional are privileged and also confidential, so these can be carried on without a confidentiality agreement.





There will inevitably be people you want or need to discuss your invention with. If you absolutely have to discuss your invention with anyone (and I really mean any living human being), such as a possible business partner, you must have that person sign a confidentiality or nondisclosure agreement (NDA) (see Appendix 6, pp.272–273, for an example) before you describe your invention to him or her.

All the confidentiality rules that relate to trade secrets also apply here. In fact, there is an overlap between trade secret and patent protection in this situation. Your invention is probably protected as a trade secret until such time as your patent application is published. You may therefore wish to carefully follow the suggestions on confidentiality outlined in the chapter on trade secrets (see pp.189–192).

Discussions with your patent professional are privileged and also confidential, so these can be carried on without a confidentiality agreement. In fact, your patent lawyer can also provide you with a suitably worded NDA.

## Keep good records

You should keep good records of your day-to-day activities when you are developing an idea into something that you would like to claim as an invention.

> **NOTE OF CAUTION! – Keep good records**
>
> The reason for this is more defensive in nature. You may be working on certain developments you have decided not to patent, but which you start to use in your business. If someone else gets a patent on these developments, he or she might sue you for infringement. If you can prove through your documentation that you were already doing what is in the plaintiff's claims, your own activities may be viewed as prior art and you are off the hook. You may also be able to show that you are entitled to a prior use right.

In my view, one of the best practices to help you keep out of this type of trouble is to keep good notes of what you are doing each day. You should sign and date every page of your notes at the end of each work session. Then have someone sign and date the page as a witness to what is on that page. You should do this as close as possible to the date that you make these entries. Otherwise you have no one to back you up as to the date on which you were already doing something. But here is where you have to be extra cautious: you should separately enter into a written agreement with your witnesses to keep any information disclosed to them in confidence. He or she should confirm that they are looking at this information only as a witness to the date that they are signing off on the pages.

### Patentability searches

Typically, patentability searches are conducted before filing a patent application. Doing so can help avoid potentially huge cost outlays and investments in your invention. It would be dispiriting to find after much time, money, and effort have been expended, that your patent application cannot succeed because your invention is not considered "new". But even if the search dredges up stuff that looks like your invention, there might still be hope.

Often you can word your claims so that what you claim is new and not obvious over the results of the search. Search results may also help you hone the wording of your own application and assist in helping to "design around" other patents still in force. The downside of doing searches is that they can be very expensive and time consuming. In fact, someone could file an application while you are still searching.

Searching, you should be aware, is also an inexact art, so there is no guarantee that a search will necessarily uncover the prior art that is

Search results may also help you hone the wording of your own application and assist in helping to "design around" other patents still in force.



most relevant to your invention. On the whole, though, my long experience dictates that the prudent route in most cases would be to consider a patentability search before filing.

In a patentability search, you essentially compare your invention against the existing prior art found during the search, that is all information disclosed to the public that predates the filing date of your patent application. Patent searchers will typically conduct such searches by using two sources: electronic patent databases and trade or technical journals and databases in the relevant area.

The two main patent databases freely accessible to the public are the **ESP@CENET** database administered by the European Patent Office (http://ep.espacenet.com), which houses 50 million patent documents, and the US Patent and Trademark Office database (http://www.uspto.gov/patft/index.html), which includes seven million patent files.

If funds are short, you may, of course, wish to conduct your own search using the above sources. However, searching does require considerable care and patience, and the above databases (in particular, **ESP@CENET**) have, by design, significant limitations, so your ability to search prior patents in detail is restricted. As a result, your own search may not be as comprehensive as one done on your behalf by a patent

**USE PATENT DATABASES**

Searching patent databases can be a very helpful resource in ways other than finding prior art: they can give you access to a wealth of technical information, including what your competitors have been up to!

professional, such as the Patent Search and Advisory Service of the UK Patent Office (commercialsearches@patent.gov.uk).

Because an inventor is often working at the cutting edge in the specific field at that moment, he or she is frequently aware of "what is out there" already. Such information can be put to good use in drafting the patent application and specification.

Patentability searches also give you access to a wealth of technical information: you may be able to identify subcomponents that have already been invented and could support the development of your invention so that you don't have to reinvent the same technology.

Patentability searches also give you access to a wealth of information: you may be able to identify subcomponents that have already been invented and could support the development of your invention.

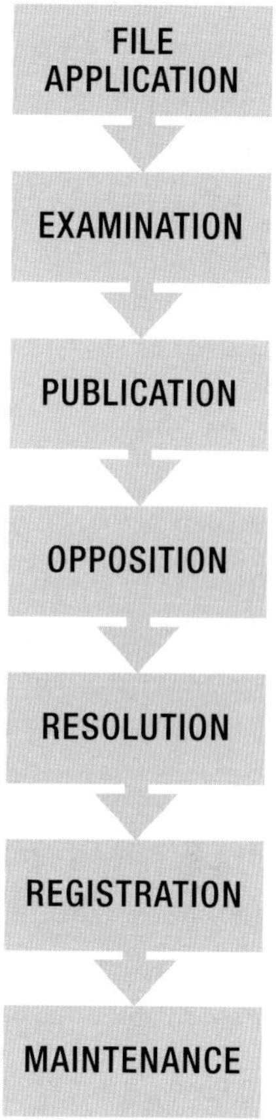

FILE APPLICATION
EXAMINATION
PUBLICATION
OPPOSITION
RESOLUTION
REGISTRATION
MAINTENANCE

Overview of the patent application process

## THE PATENT APPLICATION PROCESS

### Filing a full patent application with claims

So here you are. All primed and prepped. Ready to present your invention to the UK Patent Office to get the big stamp and ribbon on your invention and ready to enter the Nobel Prize for Science. Not so! Sorry, your work has just begun.

As I previously explained, in order to file your patent application, you have to provide a detailed description, which is essentially a written explanation of your invention. This is known as the "specification". Generally, you also need drawings.

The Patent Office has very detailed rules for drawings. Shop drawings or even technical blueprints will not work. You should use a good patent draftsperson who can prepare the drawings under the guidance of your patent professional.

The specification and drawings are followed by the claims. I can't stress enough how important your claims will be. They are at the heart of any patent, since they define the scope of protection and exclusivity provided by the patent. Your claims are legal statements typically

**TIP**

**WORK TOGETHER WITH YOUR PATENT PROFESSIONAL**

I would advise you to keep a very close watch on the drafting of the patent specification. In my experience, the best patent specifications are usually a close joint effort between the inventor and the patent professional.



captured in single sentences. They pinpoint and define your invention by describing its distinctive technical features. It is very important that the claims be extremely carefully written – they must be crystal clear, concise, and consistent with one another.

In a dispute involving your patent, the meaning of one single word in the claims could be the crucial factor in determining whether your patent is valid or invalid due to some prior patent out there or a prior disclosure you made.

Usually the claims start with a broad claim that casts the inventor's net of protection as wide as possible while still avoiding all known prior art. The broad claim is normally followed by narrower claims, which should lead to stronger claims against any prior-art references. These claims recite additional features about your invention.

!

**NOTE OF CAUTION! –** Phrasing your claims

The clarity of your claims is equally important to put everyone else on notice as to precisely what they may or may not do to avoid infringing your patent. A simple word, or the way the words in your claim are phrased, could make the difference between whether a competitor's product infringes your patent or not.

A simple word, or the way the words in your claim are phrased, could make the difference between whether a competitor's product infringes your patent or not.





**Abstract** A short summary of the essential technical aspects of your invention in the form of an abstract is also required. It enables others to obtain quick information on your invention when searching.

**Invention disclosure** You know your invention in detail. Your patent professional does not. As a practical matter, the best way to proceed in preparing the patent specification is for the inventor to first prepare an invention disclosure for the patent professional. Since the inventor knows his or her invention in detail, he or she is in the best position to describe the invention. The invention disclosure need not be overly detailed but should be sufficiently specific to convey the full nature of the invention. Keep in mind that detailed drawings are almost always required. Patent professionals will then use your invention disclosure to turn your description of the invention into "patentese" in order to draft the patent specification.

**LEGAL TEST** – Sufficient disclosure

The patent specifications must have a detailed enough description of the invention with drawings so that the invention is sufficiently disclosed. "Sufficient", according to patent law, means that someone "skilled in the art" in the relevant field (our fictional person mentioned above with an average level of skill) should be able to follow the invention.

**IS YOUR PATENT COMMERCIALLY VIABLE?**

Patents are by far the most expensive form of intellectual property. Patent registrations are expensive to obtain and patent litigation is one of the most costly forms of litigation (especially in the US). For instance, big pharmaceutical companies often continue court battles after patents have expired in anticipation of huge damage awards running into billions of dollars. So it makes real sense for you at the start of your patent process to take a hard look at the commercial prospects of your invention to fully assess the risk/reward ratio. You may wish to consider the following factors in weighing up the pros and cons:

- Is there a need for your invention in the market?
- What does the analysis on competitors and their products reveal?
- What is the best timing for releasing your product? Inventions often fail because their introductions are either premature or too late.
- How cost-effective will your invention be to produce?
- Are there potential strategic investors who will fund the development of your invention?

These and similar commercial issues should be seriously reviewed before taking the first step to making the financial outlay to support the filing of a patent application.

Invention promotion companies may be willing to undertake a market feasibility study of your invention in the UK. Be careful, as some of them may be less than reputable. If you are interested in using an invention promotion company, I suggest you consult the DTI's Consumer Direct website for valuable guidance in this potentially treacherous area at www.consumerdirect.gov.uk.

### Patent or trade secret?

Before you grab your jacket and run out the door to see a patent professional, pause for at least a moment to think about whether it makes more sense to keep your invention as a trade secret (see the chapter on trade secrets, pp.182–193).

While a patent will give you the right to prevent the competition from using your invention, that right does not last forever. In most cases, the commercial importance of your invention will be outdated before the patent expires. But, if your invention is of the type that people will want to use or exploit for decades, and it is of the type that people cannot reverse engineer, it might make sense to treat it as a trade secret. Think of the **COCA-COLA** formula. It was never patented, and only a few people know exactly what goes into the carbonated beverage to give it that famous **COCA-COLA** taste.

Taking the trade secret route may give you a competitive advantage, as trade secret protection is not limited to the patent term of 20 years. Moreover, the cost involved in trade secret protection is substantially less than obtaining and maintaining a patent. Also, you should carefully analyse whether your invention overlaps or may be "bundled" with other forms of intellectual property.

## Proceeding with your patent application

You have taken care of the basics. Along with the help of your patent professional, you have done your patentability searches, drafted your patent application, and filed your patent application at the UK Patent Office. Be prepared: this is where the difficult part starts.

### Official Actions

You will now enter into a dialogue with your Patent Examiner at the UK Patent Office through what are called Official Actions. The Examiner will typically question different aspects of your patent application and you may have to argue in support of the "novelty" and "nonobviousness" of your invention as well as possibly amend your claims. This process often lasts for years (generally between one and three years). Don't despair – this is bog standard normal and happens to virtually everybody.

TIP

**SELECT THE BEST PROFESSIONAL**

Selecting the best patent professional to persuade the Examiner of the merits of your application is a big plus and can significantly ease your way through the application process. Consult www.cipa.org.uk for a choice of patent professionals. I have found the Examiners at the UK Patent Office to be, on the whole, very professional, friendly, and helpful and the office is very accessible. As with all good things in life, everything starts with communication. Work with the Examiner rather than against him or her.

As with all good things in life, everything starts with communication. Work with the Examiner, not against him or her.

**What to claim as your invention** This is where you will have an opportunity to tweak your claims or argue with the Examiner. If the claims in your application are drafted too broadly, in order to cover a wide range of technology, you will likely encounter more obstacles from the Examiner than if you start with narrower claims. It's tempting to limit your claims in order to have your patent application allowed. But often it is better to file written arguments to the Examiner explaining why what you claim is different from prior materials. This is the delicate balance that patent professionals are trained for. And the more they understand your true invention, the better prepared they will be to decide when to argue and how to scale back your claims. This back and forth can go on for a bit. Don't lose heart, stay cool, and persevere – most patent applicants face obstacles.

Don't lose heart, stay cool, and persevere – most patent applicants face obstacles.

If you are keen to extend your patent to other countries, it is worthwhile knowing that there are various international treaties to facilitate this process.



**International extension**

If you are keen to extend your patent to other countries, it is worthwhile knowing that there are various international treaties (such as the Paris Convention, the European Patent Convention, and the Patent Cooperation Treaty "PCT") to facilitate this process. The European Patent is a particularly cost-efficient procedural tool for extending patent protection to different European countries.

The Paris Convention allows you to wait one year before deciding where to extend your patent internationally, and, by filing a single international or PCT application, this decision can be put off for a further 18 months. Taking this extra time allows you to better assess the merits and potential value of your invention before deciding to incur the relatively significant costs of international patent extensions. The PCT application must be followed by national patent applications in those countries where patent rights are desired. The PCT procedure entails a number of advantages (including cost advantages) where a national resident of a PCT member country wishes to file multiple corresponding applications in other PCT member countries.

On the big day when you receive your Patent Registration Certificate, pop a bottle of champagne. After all the hard work you deserve it. But don't forget to pay your yearly renewal fees!

> **NOTE OF CAUTION! –** Fees
> You have to pay maintenance fees during the life of your patent, or it will die a premature death. The maximum life expectancy of your patent will be 20 years from the date you filed your full application with claims. There are no extensions, unless you have a friend in Parliament.



## HOW CAN I GENERATE REVENUES FROM MY PATENT?

A single inventor will often find that it is very costly to manufacture or distribute a newly invented product alone. Often the best way to exploit your invention is to hook an 800-pound gorilla company that shows an interest in the invention. You can either sell your invention and assign your patent to such a company for a lump sum, or license your patent against a royalty income stream to a business partner. Carefully weigh all the pros and cons of self manufacture, selling, and licensing, but don't forget to include patent maintenance and potential defence costs in the equation.

## WHEN DOES SOMEONE INFRINGE MY PATENT?

It is not at all uncommon for competitors to copy an invention before the patent has even issued. You can determine whether the claims as you have worded them cover what your competitor is doing. If they do not, there may still be some time to alter your claims to pick up what the infringer is doing. However, until a patent actually issues, you cannot sue anyone to stop him or her from using, making, or selling what you claim as your invention. There are procedures in the Patent Office where you can expedite your application if you believe that your invention has been copied. Sometimes a demand letter can be sent to your competitor before your patent issues, but it would have to be very carefully worked out with your patent professional to ensure you do not run afoul of the

**TIP**

**THINK ABOUT OPPORTUNITIES FOR CROSS-LICENSING**

Sometimes your competition not only infringes your rights but actually introduces a product with some improvements. This can put you in a bind. You know that consumers would rather have your opponent's product than yours. But your opponent needs a licence from you to sell the product, even with the improvement, because the product incorporates the product you claim. And if your competitor has received a patent on the improved product, you can be precluded from making that improvement yourself. This is where a cross-licensing arrangement can come into play. Cross-licensing opportunities come up even when there is no litigation. Think of the successful Sony and Samsung venture.

patent law that prohibits the making of unfounded threats. However, this may help you work out some form of settlement so that, by the time your patent issues, the offending product is off the market or you have a licence in place. You can warn your competitor that you are in the process of receiving a patent and that you are prepared to initiate litigation as soon as the patent issues. If the application has been published, you can send a copy of your claims so your competition knows it is in trouble.

If instead you wait until your patent issues to send letters or an infringement occurs after your patent issues, you still have to make sure your claims cover what your competition is doing. If you are willing to settle for a reasonable royalty, your opponent might be agreeable to something. But this is where I need to give you a reality check. Patent litigation is incredibly expensive and can sometimes drag on forever. It also takes you and your employees away from your business – you end up spending a lot of time with your lawyers. Also, the first thing most opponents will attempt to do is to invalidate your patent by

attacking its merits. Needless to say, having a skilled lawyer at this stage is of enormous assistance. Settling with your opponent is very often the sensible outcome in many a patent dispute.

**SHOULD YOU SUE?**

When you send a letter to an opponent, he or she will generally respond with the types of arguments I have outlined above. But in some cases an aggressive opponent will use your letter as a basis to start a lawsuit against you. You might ask, "how can that happen? These are *my* rights that have been infringed!" Well, it can.

The opponent can ask a court to declare that your patent is invalid or that your claims are not infringed. For this reason, some patent owners choose to sue people before they even send a warning letter.

Consult with your lawyer carefully on this strategy. But remember, just because you own a patent does not mean that you cannot be sued. Also, beware: your letter will have to be carefully worded to avoid a claim of groundless threats of patent infringement by the person who receives your letter.

# CHAPTER 6
# intellectual property

## BUNDLING YOUR INTELLECTUAL PROPERTY

I have already referred to the concept of **BUNDLING** your various **INTELLECTUAL PROPERTY RIGHTS** together in the chapters on trade marks, copyright, design rights, trade secrets, and patents. In essence, it means that you should look at your new **INTELLECTUAL CREATION** from a **HOLISTIC** perspective. You may have rights to more than one form of **INTELLECTUAL PROPERTY**, and these can be **BUNDLED** together to help strengthen your arsenal. The more **INTELLECTUAL PROPERTY RIGHTS** you have established in your **NEW CREATION**, the better are the chances of an infringer being caught transgressing one of the boundaries. Believe me, in any **INTELLECTUAL PROPERTY** conflict, you need strong and varied weapons – whether you are involved in the full-scale war of an infringement suit or the more subtle art of settlement negotiations.

Believe me, if you get into any intellectual property battles, you will need strong and varied protection.



Whether you know it or not, you are making business decisions when you choose not to pursue intellectual property protection. You might be passing up opportunities that will not be there if you fail to take certain steps from the beginning. Remember the 10-ton weight with the one-year clock ticking over your invention? And what if somebody else files a trade mark application for a mark similar to the one you plan to use but haven't got around to filing yet? That could force you to change your entire branding scheme or pay that person a lot of money to get out of the way.

By getting on file and taking other steps to protect your new creations, the better the chances of an infringer being caught or just staying away in the first place. Believe me, if you get into any intellectual property battles, you will need strong and varied protection. This is true whether you are involved in the full-scale war of an infringement suit or the more subtle art of settlement negotiations.

Now, I hope you can look back at the **PANERAI** branded watch example on p.41 and appreciate how a single item can be protected by different categories and layers of intellectual property. At the beginning of the book I showed a few of the more obvious examples. Those are repeated here, but the list has grown to show how the possibilities are endless.

At least 17 forms of intellectual property could be available for such a watch:

- Trade mark rights in the house mark **PANERAI**.
- Trade mark rights in the name **LUMINOR MARINA**.
- Trade mark rights in the three-dimensional product design for the watch.
- Trade mark rights in the three-dimensional product design for the crown lock.
- Design rights in the watch-face design.
- Design rights in the watch-case design.
- Design rights in the crown lock.
- Design rights in the bezel.
- Design rights in the watch package.
- Trade secret rights in the manner of assembling the watch mechanism.
- Trade secret rights in the manner of manufacturing some of the parts that cannot be reversed engineered.
- Patent rights in the new and improved features of the watch mechanism.
- Patent rights in the way the watch box is made.
- Copyright in the design drawings of the watch.
- Copyright in advertisements that feature the watch.
- Rights of publicity that need to be cleared if any personalities are used to endorse or promote the watch.
- Trade name rights in the company name **OFFICINE PANERAI**.

TIP

## ANALYSE YOUR INTELLECTUAL PROPERTY

The **PANERAI** watch example (pp.240–241) represents a fairly standard example of the number of intellectual property rights that may be embodied in a single creation. Following the guidance in the chapters on trade marks, copyright, design rights, trade secrets, and patents, go through a quick checklist to see whether your new intellectual creation qualifies for protection in more than one area (also see the summary on pp.38–39). Once you know whether your creation qualifies, follow the steps outlined in the different chapters to evidence your proof that you are first in time, first in right.





As you can see from the example on p.240–241, a seemingly straightforward product like a watch, its packaging, and its advertising campaign can be protected by intellectual property in various ways. Trade marks, design rights, and patents are all spilling over. Trade secrets and know-how play an important role and copyright is there to protect the artistic expression on the packaging and advertisements. At the manufacturing level, trade secrets and patents protect the manufacturing equipment and packaging processes, and there are copyright and further patents for the software that tracks inventory.

If the list of possibilities for bundling your intellectual property starts to look endless to you, it is. The companies and individuals involved in the creation, design, manufacture, and distribution of consumer products have substantial investments in place. Whether you are buying a tube of **COLGATE** toothpaste off the shelf at a **BOOTS** store or downloading the newest **GREEN DAY** release for your **IPOD** player, you can be assured that there have been a lot of people involved to get these products and services delivered to you so that you know you are getting the best product for your money. And so a long list of intellectual property rights is available to protect the labours of these people and companies.

## HOW TO GET THE MOST OUT OF YOUR INTELLECTUAL PROPERTY PROFESSIONAL

Here are a few thoughts on how to get the most out of the intellectual property professionals who can assist you in your quest. Keep in mind that intellectual property law is one of the most dynamic and constantly changing areas of law. Like many other areas of law, it is also rife with potholes and loopholes. Furthermore, it is a highly specialized area. There are a number of different intellectual property specialists, including intellectual property barristers, intellectual property solicitors, corporate and commercial lawyers, trade mark agents, and patent agents. I suggest you carefully select the best specialist for your situation.

### ▶ Intellectual property barristers

They are the heavies – the hired guns who will usually litigate and present your case in court. They may also provide you with opinions on a particular intellectual property case.

### ▶ Intellectual property solicitors

They are the facilitators. Their role is to advise you on intellectual property conflicts. They will also assist the barristers in preparing for litigation. Solicitors will, in the case of settlement negotiations, help you draft and settle a particular matter. In addition, they are the ones who deal with various contracts such as licensing and the transfer of intellectual property. They can also help you set up an appropriate intellectual property ownership structure. Some solicitor firms will provide assistance with filing and other formalities in helping establish evidence of ownership.

### ▶ Corporate and commercial lawyers

Corporate and commercial lawyers who do not specialize in intellectual property often dabble in this area. My advice to you would be to proceed with caution. Asking a commercial lawyer with limited experience in the field of intellectual property to sort out your intellectual property issues is a little like asking a dermatologist to remove your tonsils. On the whole, I would suggest you consult with a specialist. It really is horses for courses.

Asking a commercial lawyer with limited experience in the field of intellectual property to sort out your intellectual property issues is a little like asking a dermatologist to remove your tonsils.

### ► Trade mark agents and patent agents

These professionals may assist you with filing applications while dealing with Official Actions and Oppositions from the UK Patent Office. In other words, they will help you conduct searches and draft the specifications of both trade mark and patent applications.

There are also various intellectual property service firms that deal with searches. Here I would suggest that you go for the one-stop approach. Rather than consult a firm to assist you with searches, and then another to deal with legal matters, it would make better sense to approach either a solicitor or agent, depending on the case, to help you with all the different issues involved.

**NOTE OF CAUTION! – Disreputable companies**

As always, a note of caution. There are firms out there who are less than reputable. Such firms will offer you a smorgasbord of all kinds of services without being properly accredited or qualified to render them. As in all walks of life, check and double check the qualifications and expertise of the intellectual property professional you select. Some listings that may assist you in this project are:

www.chambersandpartners.com
www.iplawdirectory.com
www.legal500.com
www.itma.org.uk
www.cipa.org.uk.

**TIP**

**ASK FOR A FULL ESTIMATE**

Ask your intellectual property professional for an upfront estimate before you start. Even filing fees, especially patent fees, can be very expensive, so make sure you get a full estimate – not only for the short term – but also for the long term. Maintenance fees in themselves may be expensive. Do as you would do with any other item in business: set up a proper budget and manage it during the different stages along with your intellectual property professional.





Cost and expense, financially and time-wise, are always important, whether you are a lone individual or a big company. Therefore, do your homework well and approach the issue of intellectual property protection the same way as you would any other service.

Even intellectual property professionals specialize amongst themselves. You often find that there are specialists who will deal only with patents and others who will deal only with trade marks. If you are dealing with more than one specialist within a firm, it is very important that you ensure that they coordinate their efforts properly. This sounds easy but, believe me, managing and coordinating the efforts of specialists isn't always a walk in the park. But, it is imperative all the same.

You may set up special entities such as limited liability companies, or corporations, or partnerships to own your intellectual property portfolio and other assets of your business. In doing so, you may bring in partners, investors, and other entities who will have a financial interest or some other type of interest in your intellectual property. The moment other people or entities start taking on one of these interests, you need to start thinking about whether your own personal interests may be different from the interests of the ownership entity and you should let your lawyer know if this is beginning to happen.

Do not take these questions personally. Polite, concise, and common-sense responses are always the best way forward.





## DEALING WITH PATENT AND TRADE MARK OFFICE EXAMINERS

Some good news. In my view, we in the UK are fortunate to have some of the most courteous, helpful, and accessible Examiners in the world. So make the most of this happy state of affairs. As mentioned in the previous chapters, the Examiner in patent and trade mark cases will communicate with you through what are called Official Actions. The key here is to establish a successful line of communication with your Examiner. Do not approach the Examiner as the enemy. I seriously suggest that you phone your Examiner and have a talk. You are sure to find the person you are dealing with to be helpful and professional. Find out what the real concern is and address it head on in a constructive way. I often find that straightforward common-sense answers prevail.

Keep in mind that it is the Examiner's job to analyse and examine your application. He or she will, therefore, raise questions in relation to the merits of your patent or trade mark application and the wording of your specifications. Do not take these questions personally. Polite, concise, and common-sense responses are always the best way forward. The examination process is a necessary hurdle to be tackled in a professional and polite manner.

## FILING INTERNATIONALLY

If you know from the outset that you will use your new intellectual property creation not only in the UK but also in other countries, you should consider an international filing programme. You may initially start off in the UK and then, if your brain baby turns out to be a huge hit, decide to expand your business to other countries. In these circumstances, you should be aware that there are a number of international intellectual property treaties that allow you to use the UK (your home country filing) as a springboard to extend to other countries.

In fact, quite a lot of work has been done by the World Intellectual Property Organization and other bodies to establish regional and international filing systems. Something to take into account when contemplating an international filing programme is the fact that certain intellectual property treaties allow you to maintain your crucial priority date in your home country when you extend your applications or registrations to other countries. But this must be done within a set time period. Some international treaties allow for a six-month period (for example, in the case of trade marks and design rights) and others allow one year (in the case of patents, which may be extended in some cases to two and a half years).

International systems usefully serve as a "one-stop shop".

Typically, when using international filing systems, your costs are reduced and you may even have the added bonus of having an expedited application procedure.

Let me illustrate this by way of an example. Let's say you would like to extend the sales of your product to some countries in Europe. Rather than file a national application in each country separately, you may wish to simply file an application covering all of the European Union at the Community Trademark Office in Alicante. Taking your product or service outside Europe is also fairly streamlined. For example, if you wish to extend your patent rights to the US, Japan, China, and a few other commercially important countries, you can make use of the International Patent Cooperation Treaty to accomplish this most effectively. These international systems usefully serve as a "one-stop shop".

After years of international bickering, I am happy to say that a number of countries have now signed up as members of these international intellectual property treaties, which in practice means that you can extend your application or registration to quite a significant number of countries. The relevant treaties are the Paris Convention, which has 167 country members, the Madrid Protocol and Agreement with 78 country members, the Hague Convention with 65 members, and the International Patent Cooperation Treaty with 132 country members.

Needless to say, how to get the best bang for your buck, the pros and cons of an international filing system, and how to make use of them in the most efficient way, should be worked through with your intellectual property professional.

## TAX AND INTELLECTUAL PROPERTY

Intellectual property has become one of the most valuable assets in today's world. And the taxman is very much aware of this fact. So be careful. If your intellectual property venture is taking off, there are some points you should take into consideration. When selling your intellectual property creation, buying someone else's, or licensing your own creation, careful tax consideration and planning will be required. Your intellectual property professional can direct you to someone who will be helpful to you on this issue. Also, if your business starts taking off in the international arena (or you plan from the outset to go global), it is advisable to receive good advice on tax-efficient intellectual property ownership structures.

## WARNINGS AND MARKINGS

You may have noticed that intellectual property owners often use warnings and markings to alert people to the ownership in their creation. The obvious legal advantage is that this gives people notice of your rights and, in some cases, may help you with your damage claims if someone else infringes your rights. Apart from legal considerations, warnings and markings are very practical and have a psychologically cautionary effect on potential infringers. In fact, they may even help people who are acting innocently and in good faith and who are otherwise unaware that you may have intellectual property rights in your creation.

### WARNINGS AND MARKINGS

Here are a few examples you may wish to consider for use on packaging, labels, or documents relating to your creation:

| | |
|---|---|
| Trade marks | ▶ **Brand™** (before your mark is registered) |
| | ▶ **Brand®** (after your mark is registered) |
| Copyright | ▶ **© 2007. John Smith. All Rights Reserved.** |
| Design rights | ▶ **Registered** (after your design is registered). |
| Patents | ▶ **Patent Pending** (while your patent application is pending). |
| | ▶ **Patented** or **Patent Registered** or **Registered** (after your patent is registered). |

TIP

**KEEP YOUR WARNINGS AND MARKINGS UP-TO-DATE**

Remember to update your intellectual property warnings and markings as the status of your intellectual property changes. Your patent professional should provide your patent number just before it issues. You should immediately begin changing your labels and other markings to show the patent number. It is very frustrating when I have spent time registering a trade mark for a client, then years later continue to see ™ rather than ® on packaging.

Use these notices whenever your mark is prominently displayed on packaging, advertisements, and promotional materials. You should use it with your logos too. The notices do not need to go after each use on your materials. That looks geeky and is usually overkill.

If there are a variety of intellectual property rights contained in a particular creation – which is often the case – you can use legends that are prominently displayed, usually on the back of packaging, on the product itself, or on labels.

**LEGENDS**

The examples will vary depending upon what type of intellectual property is involved but here are three, just to give you some ideas:

- XYZ and the XYZ Logo are trade marks. All unauthorized use is prohibited. © 2007 John Smith. All Rights Reserved.
- Patent Pending. XYZ® is a registered trade mark and the XYZ logo is a trade mark. All unauthorized use is prohibited.
- Patent Nos. 123, 456, and 789, Design Right Nos. 123, 456, and 789. © 2002, 2004, 2007. Mary Doe.

## INTELLECTUAL PROPERTY CONFLICTS AND LITIGATION

Registries around the world are becoming ever more cluttered as people become increasingly aware of and assertive in their intellectual property rights. Many more conflicts and a rise in litigation have been the result. At some point you may very well find yourself either on the sending or on the receiving end of an intellectual property warning letter. This is part and parcel of intellectual property enforcement. It can be truly nerve-racking at times but mostly it is simply irritating. Make peace with the knowledge that you will not always have a smooth ride. However, your intellectual property professional will navigate you

through these treacherous waters and, if common sense prevails, you should be fine.

Registries around the world are becoming ever more cluttered as people become increasingly aware of and assertive in their intellectual property rights.

TIP

**EXERCISE RESTRAINT**

Most cases are brought for commercial and legal reasons, but at some points during the course of the legal proceedings the whole process will become unavoidably emotional. Parties become entrenched in their positions and emotions run high. This is when you approach what I consider the point of no return. Try to practise restraint. Common sense often can, and should, prevail in these situations to determine whether settlement would be a viable and more sensible option.



Having your intellectual property stolen is traumatic. I know – it has happened to me as well. Not only have your intellectual property rights been infringed, but there is a sense of personal violation involved. The immediate reaction is often to contemplate litigation. Allow me to quote my father, who, after 40 years of law practice, gave me the following advice: "When your client is looking for blood, settlement seems tame. But always, always try to settle first. Only if you've tried everything reasonable to settle out of court and failed, do you take off the gloves. And then: to battle".

So turn the other cheek before you think eye for an eye. Settling out of court will save you enormous heartache. It will save you outrageous expenses in legal fees but also, crucially, valuable management time. Lost management time is an opportunity lost that could have been spent productively on running your business and developing your creation. Bear in mind too that in the UK the general rule in litigation is that the loser pays all fees. In other words, the party that has lost the case will have to pay not only for his or her own lawyer's fees but also those of the winning party – a double wallop. If you do, however, end up in court, you may earn some Brownie points if you show that you made genuine attempts at settlement. In my experience, mediation is a very useful method of resolving conflicts quickly and efficiently. A mediator is a neutral referee (typically an intellectual property professional) who

In the UK the general rule in litigation is that the loser pays all fees.







serves as an objective and mutual go-between for both sides to solve the conflict professionally in a swift and inexpensive way. Arbitration, which is a more formalized version, might also achieve the same result.

Of course, the other side may show no interest in being reasonable and common sense may not be a concept within their frame of reference. In these cases, the second part of my father's advice applies: take off the gloves and to battle. Arm yourself with the best possible team. Pick your intellectual property litigators carefully and good luck!

**ONE FINAL THOUGHT (HUMOUR ME, I'M A LAWYER. I CAN'T HELP IT)**

"It is easy to copy; difficult to create. That is why the intellectual products of creative minds are valued so highly and poached so consistently." Anonymous

Along the way, the laws have developed to protect your inventions, designs and works of art. Other laws have developed to protect your trade marks and trade secrets. The laws are on your side, and so are our society and culture. Let your creative spirit run wild, and make sure to protect your creations along the way!

# appendices



These appendices are here to help and guide you, but they are not a substitute for expert legal help. Suggestions may not apply in all situations and modifications may be required. Neither the publisher nor the author accepts any responsibility for any losses that may arise from the use or adaptation of these sample agreements.

These documents are just examples. You should work closely with your intellectual property lawyer on any document before it is signed. This will ensure that all your rights are protected.

## CLASSIFICATION OF GOODS AND SERVICES

The following headings give general information about the types of goods and services which belong to each class. Goods are in Classes 1 to 34. Services are in Classes 35 to 45. The list is not complete and is merely a guide to the classes that may be required. The UK Patent Office has an excellent search tool to help you select specific identifications at http://www.patent.gov.uk/tm/dbase/goodsclass/index.htm



### Goods

*Class 1* Chemicals used in industry, science, and photography, as well as in agriculture, horticulture, and forestry; unprocessed artificial resins, unprocessed plastics; manures; fire-extinguishing compositions; tempering and soldering preparations; chemical substances for preserving foodstuffs; tanning substances; adhesives used in industry.

*Class 2* Paints, varnishes, lacquers; preservatives against rust and against deterioration of wood; colorants; mordants; raw natural resins; metals in foil and powder form for painters, decorators, printers, and artists.

*Class 3* Bleaching preparations and other substances for laundry use; cleaning, polishing, scouring, and abrasive preparations; soaps; perfumery, essential oils, cosmetics, hair lotions; dentifrices.

*Class 4* Industrial oils and greases; lubricants; dust-absorbing, wetting, and binding compositions; fuels (including motor spirit) and illuminants; candles and wicks for lighting.

*Class 5* Pharmaceutical and veterinary preparations; sanitary preparations for medical purposes; dietetic substances adapted for medical use, food for babies; plasters, materials for dressings; material for stopping teeth, dental wax; disinfectants; preparations for destroying vermin; fungicides, herbicides.

*Class 6* Common metals and their alloys; metal building materials; transportable buildings of metal; materials of metal for railway tracks; nonelectric cables and wires of common metal; ironmongery, small items of metal hardware; pipes and tubes of metal; safes; goods of common metal not included in other classes; ores.

*Class 7* Machines and machine tools; motors and engines (except for land vehicles); machine coupling and transmission components (except for land vehicles); agricultural implements other than hand-operated; incubators for eggs.

*Class 8* Hand tools and implements (hand operated); cutlery; side arms; razors.

*Class 9* Scientific, nautical, surveying, photographic, cinematographic, optical, weighing, measuring, signalling, checking (supervision), life-saving, and teaching apparatus and instruments; apparatus and instruments for conducting, switching, transforming, accumulating, regulating, or controlling electricity; apparatus for recording, transmission, or reproduction of sound or images; magnetic data carriers, recording discs; automatic vending machines and mechanisms for coin-operated apparatus; cash registers; calculating machines, data-processing equipment, and computers; fire-extinguishing apparatus.

*Class 10* Surgical, medical, dental, and veterinary apparatus and instruments, artificial limbs, eyes, and teeth; orthopaedic articles; suture materials.

*Class 11* Apparatus for lighting, heating, steam generating, cooking, refrigerating, drying, ventilating, water supply, and sanitary purposes.

*Class 12* Vehicles; apparatus for locomotion by land, air, or water.

*Class 13* Firearms; ammunition and projectiles, explosives; fireworks.

*Class 14* Precious metals and their alloys and goods in precious metals or coated therewith not included in other classes; jewellery, precious stones; horological and chronometric instruments.

*Class 15* Musical instruments.

*Class 16* Paper, cardboard, and goods made from these materials not included in other classes; printed matter; book-binding material; photographs; stationery; adhesives for stationery or household purposes; artists' materials; paint brushes; typewriters and office requisites (except furniture); instructional and teaching material (except apparatus); plastic materials for packaging (not included in other classes); printers' type; printing blocks.

*Class 17* Rubber, gutta-percha, gum, asbestos, mica, and goods made from these materials and not included in other classes; plastics in extruded form for use in manufacture; packing, stopping, and insulating materials; flexible pipes not of metal.

*Class 18* Leather and imitations of leather, and goods made of these materials and not included in other classes; animal skins, hides; trunks and travelling bags; umbrellas, parasols, and walking sticks; whips, harness, and saddlery.

*Class 19* Building materials (nonmetallic); nonmetallic rigid pipes for building; asphalt, pitch, and bitumen; nonmetallic transportable buildings; monuments not of metal.

*Class 20* Furniture, mirrors, picture frames; goods (not included in other classes) of wood, cork, reed, cane, wicker, horn, bone, ivory, whalebone, shell, amber, mother-of-pearl, meerschaum, and substitutes for all these materials, or of plastics.

*Class 21* Household or kitchen utensils and containers (not of precious metal or coated therewith); combs and sponges; brushes (except paint brushes); brush-making materials; articles for cleaning purposes; steel wool; unworked or semi-worked glass (except glass used in building); glassware, porcelain, and earthenware not included in other classes.

*Class 22* Ropes, string, nets, tents, awnings, tarpaulins, sails, sacks, and bags not included in other classes; padding and stuffing materials (except of rubber or plastics); raw fibrous textile materials.

*Class 23* Yarns and threads for textile use.

*Class 24* Textiles and textile goods not included in other classes; bed and table covers.

*Class 25* Clothing, footwear, headgear.

*Class 26* Lace and embroidery, ribbons and braid; buttons, hooks and eyes, pins and needles; artificial flowers.

*Class 27* Carpets, rugs, mats, and matting, linoleum and other materials for covering existing floors; wall hangings (nontextile).

*Class 28* Games and playthings; gymnastic and sporting articles not included in other classes; decorations for Christmas trees.

*Class 29* Meat, fish, poultry, and game; meat extracts; preserved, dried, and cooked fruits and vegetables; jellies, jams, fruit sauces; eggs, milk, and milk products; edible oils and fats.

*Class 30* Coffee, tea, cocoa, sugar, rice, tapioca, sago, artificial coffee; flour and preparations made from cereals, bread, pastry, and confectionery, ices; honey, treacle; yeast, baking powder; salt, mustard; vinegar, sauces (condiments); spices; ice.

*Class 31* Agricultural, horticultural, and forestry products and grains not included in other classes; live animals; fresh fruits and vegetables, seeds, natural plants, and flowers; foodstuffs for animals; malt.

*Class 32* Beers; mineral and aerated waters and other nonalcoholic drinks; fruit drinks and fruit juices; syrups and other preparations for making beverages.

*Class 33* Alcoholic beverages (except beers).

*Class 34* Tobacco; smokers' articles; matches.

## Services

*Class 35* Advertising; business management; business administration; office functions.

*Class 36* Insurance; financial affairs; monetary affairs; real estate affairs.

*Class 37* Building construction; repair; installation services.

*Class 38* Telecommunications.

*Class 39* Transport; packaging and storage of goods; travel arrangement.

*Class 40* Treatment of materials.

*Class 41* Education; providing of training; entertainment; sporting and cultural activities.

*Class 42* Scientific and technological services and research and design relating thereto; industrial analysis and research services; design and development of computer hardware and software; legal services.

*Class 43* Services for providing food and drink; temporary accommodation.

*Class 44* Medical services; veterinary services; hygienic and beauty care for human beings or animals; agriculture, horticulture, and forestry services.

*Class 45* Personal and social services rendered by others to meet the needs of individuals; security services for the protection of property and individuals.

## EXAMPLE OF A COEXISTENCE AGREEMENT IN MULTIPLE COUNTRIES

This Agreement is made the [*insert day*] day of [*insert month*] 20[ ], by and between X [*insert individual's name and citizenship, or corporate name and country*] located at [*insert address*] ("X") and Y, a company incorporated under the laws of [*insert individual's name and citizenship, or corporate name and country*], located at [*insert address*] ("Y").

WHEREAS, X has adopted and used the mark [*insert trade mark*] in good faith in various countries of the world and primarily in respect of [*insert description of goods or services*]; and

WHEREAS, Y, has adopted and used the mark [*insert trade mark*] in good faith in various countries of the world primarily in relation to [*insert description of goods or services*]; and

WHEREAS X has objected to Y's registration of [*insert trade mark*] in [*insert country*]; and

WHEREAS Y has objected to X's registration of [*insert trade mark*] in [*insert country*]; and

WHEREAS, both parties desire to develop and pursue their respective businesses and to avoid any confusion between their respective marks;

NOW THEREFORE, in consideration of the mutual covenants contained herein and for other good and valuable consideration, the receipt and sufficiency of which is mutually acknowledged, the parties agree as follows:

1. Y will not object to the use by X of the trade mark [*insert X's trade mark*] in [*insert country*] in relation to [*insert specific goods/services*];

2. X will not object to the use by Y of the trade mark [*insert Y's trade mark*] in [*insert country*] in relation to [*insert specific goods/services*];

3. X will withdraw any oppositions filed against Y's trade mark applications within 14 days following the signing of this Agreement;

4. Y will withdraw any oppositions filed against X's trade mark applications within 14 days following the signing of this Agreement;

5. The parties will assist one another in obtaining registrations for their respective marks for their respective goods of interest as set out in clauses 1 and 2 respectively above in any country of the world and will provide each other with letters of consent where necessary;

6. This Agreement will be binding upon and inure to the benefit of the parties, their affiliates, successors, and assigns. The term affiliate means any corporation, partnership, licensee, or other entity that owns or controls, is owned or controlled by, or is under the common control with, a party to this Agreement;

7. This Agreement shall be governed by and interpreted exclusively in accordance with the laws of England and Wales. In respect of any dispute concerning this Agreement, the parties hereby submit to the exclusive jurisdiction of the English Courts;

8. This Agreement does not constitute either party hereto the agent of the other party or create a partnership, joint venture, or similar relationship between the parties;

9. This Agreement shall commence on the date first above written and shall continue without limit of period.

Executed for and on behalf of X

By:

Name:

Title:

Date:

Executed for and on behalf of Y

By:

Name:

Title:

Date:

## EXAMPLE OF A LETTER OF APPOINTMENT OF QUALITY CONTROL INSPECTOR

As you know, the above trade marks are registered in the name of [*insert name of owner of trade marks*]. They are licensed to [*insert name of licensee*], which uses the trade marks in relation to the promotion of goods, services, or in respect of events.

You have been charged with the responsibility for maintaining control over the quality of the goods, services, promotions, and/or events and you are asked to ensure that they conform to standards laid down by us, which standards will be conveyed to you from time to time. Please obtain regular samples of the use of the marks in relation to the goods, services, promotions, and/or events, and conduct such inspections and tests as will ensure maintenance of the required standards. Any failure to maintain such standards is to be reported to us immediately.

## EXAMPLE OF A CREATOR'S STATUTORY DECLARATION

IN THE MATTER of the verification of the date of creation of certain copyright works

STATUTORY DECLARATION OF

[*Fill in your name*]

I, [*fill in your name*] of [*fill in your address*]

DO SOLEMNLY AND SINCERELY DECLARE as follows:

1. I am [*a designer/other appropriate description of your job title*]. I am a citizen of [*fill in your country of citizenship*] and my domicile is [*fill in your address*].

2. On [*date*] I produced a series of designs and drawings for a [*insert description of the product/work*]. Copies of these drawings are now produced and shown to me marked [*insert your initials and number each individual drawing e.g. ML1, ML2*] (the "Drawings").

3. I confirm that the Drawings are all original works created by me and are not copies or substantial copies of any other work.

4. I further confirm that the signature and date which appears on each of the Drawings contained in exhibit [*insert your initials and the number you have given each document e.g. ML1*] was applied by me.

AND I MAKE THIS SOLEMN DECLARATION conscientiously believing the same to be true by virtue of the provisions of the Statutory Declarations Act 1835. Declared by [*insert your name*]

At [*insert place where you make declaration*] [Please note that you need to make this Declaration in front of a Notary/Commissioner of Oaths/Solicitor. Please ensure that you physically attach the individual drawings to the individual exhibit cover sheets.]

This [*insert date*] day of [*insert month*] 20[ ]

Before me,
Commissioner for Oaths/Solicitor/Notary Public

IN THE MATTER of the verification of the date of creation of certain designs

STATUTORY DECLARATION OF
[*Fill in your name*]

This is the Exhibit marked [*insert the number you have given each document e.g. ML1*] referred to in the Statutory Declaration of [*fill in your name*]

This [*insert date*] day of [*insert month*] 20[ ]

Before me,
Commissioner for Oaths/Solicitor/Notary Public

## EXAMPLE OF AN ASSIGNMENT OF COPYRIGHT AGREEMENT

This agreement is made this [*insert date*] day of [*insert month*] 20[ ], between [*insert name of person, their country of citizenship, and year of birth or the name of the company assigning copyright*] (hereinafter known as Assignor) and [*insert name of person/company to whom copyright is being given*] (hereinafter known as Assignee).

This will confirm our understanding with respect to the copyright ownership in respect of the various materials that have been prepared by Assignor attached as Annex "A" (hereinafter the "Works") [*ensure you include in the Annex a full description of all the relevant copyright works to be assigned and copies of the same*] and the assignment of such ownership to Assignee.

In consideration of the appropriate payment for such assistance and other valuable consideration paid by Assignee to Assignor (and receipt of which is hereby acknowledged by the Assignor), Assignor hereby transfers, conveys, and assigns to Assignee all copyright and rights in the nature of copyright or rights under copyright in the Works throughout the world for the original terms of copyright and all renewals and extensions thereof, together with all rights to sue for previous and subsequent infringements of copyright and to recover damages in respect of all such acts of infringement of the copyright in the Works, together with the right to make such kinds of uses and adaptations thereof and changes therein as Assignee in its sole discretion may determine.

TIP

**MORAL RIGHTS**

Often, if you are the assignee you will not want the assignor to be able to assert any moral rights. In these cases, the assignee should try to get the assignor to waive the moral rights with language such as, "Assignor hereby waives the right to enforce any and all moral rights in the work". This is regarded as quite normal practice in the UK.



The Assignor shall execute any and all further instruments and otherwise cooperate and assist Assignee with any and all actions that may be necessary or reasonably requested to effectuate this assignment and transfer and maintain the continued protection of each Work subject hereto.

Signed this [*insert date*] day of [*insert month*] 20[ ]

Assignor Name:

Assignee Name:

## EXAMPLE OF A NONDISCLOSURE AGREEMENT/ CONFIDENTIALITY AGREEMENT

To: [*insert name of person/company receiving the confidential information*] ("the Recipient")

In consideration of [*insert name of person/company disclosing the confidential information*] ("the Originator") disclosing certain information relating to the project ("the Information"), the Recipient undertakes:

1. to use the Information solely for the purpose of commenting or advising / on the [*insert description/name of project*] project;

2. to keep the Information confidential until the Information comes into the public domain through no act or default on the part of the Recipient or the Recipient's agents or employees;

3. not to disclose the Information directly or indirectly to any person unless prior written consent is obtained from the Originator to discuss the Information with Recipient's other employees or agents;

4. to keep the Information and all information generated by the Recipient based thereon separate from all documents and other information of the Recipient and under the Recipient's effective control at its usual place of business;

5. not to make any copy, note, or record of the Information without the prior written consent of the Originator and that all copies, notes, and records of the Information made by the Recipient will be clearly marked "Strictly Confidential";

6. to return the Information and all copies, notes, and records of the Information to the Originator immediately upon request and expunge all information from any computer, word processor, or other device containing the Information;

7. the restrictions herein provided shall not apply with respect to Information otherwise known by the Recipient, or Information that was or becomes part of the public domain without breach of this Agreement by the Recipient or which was independently developed by the Recipient or is required to be disclosed under law, provided the Recipient notifies the Originator prior to making any such disclosure;

8. that it acknowledges and agrees that because of the unique nature of the Information, Originator will suffer irreparable harm in the event that Recipient fails to comply with its obligations hereunder and that monetary damages will be inadequate to compensate Originator for a breach of this Agreement. Accordingly, Recipient agrees that Originator will have the right to seek immediate injunctive relief to enforce Recipient's obligations contained herein.

Signed by: [*insert name of Recipient*]
On behalf of:
Date:

# NOTES

# NOTES

## PUBLISHER'S ACKNOWLEDGMENTS

Dorling Kindersley would like to thank Fran Vargo for picture research and Romaine Werblow in the DK picture library. Thanks also go to Patricia Carroll for copyediting and indexing, and Corinne Asghar, Ann Baggaley, Hannah Charlick, and Tara Woolnough for proofreading and editorial assistance.

Many thanks also to all the organizations that gave permission to reproduce their intellectual property: Apple Computer Inc., Chloe International, the Coca-Cola Company, Dyson Ltd, Eastman Kodak Company, H.J. Heinz Company Ltd, the Jean-Paul Gaultier Company, KFC Corporation, the Michelin Tyre Public Limited Company, Officine Panerai, Penguin Books Ltd, the Shaolin Temple, Shell Oil Company, Starcknetwork, and Transport for London.

## ABOUT THE AUTHOR

**Frederick Mostert** is Chief Intellectual Property Counsel of the Richemont Group which includes Cartier, Montblanc, and Chloe. He is Past President of the International Trademark Association and a Guest Professor at Peking University. He is a solicitor of England and Wales and a member of the New York Bar where he was in private practice with Shearman and Sterling and Fross Zelnick. He is principal author and editor of the book *Famous and Well-Known Marks – An International Analysis.* He has written widely on the subject of intellectual property and has been cited in judgments in the High Court in the United Kingdom and the United States Federal Court. He has received a World Leaders' European Award for "Best Achievement in Intellectual Property Management".

He was a member of the World Intellectual Property Organization's Panel of Experts on the Internet Domain Name Process and serves on various advisory boards including the McCarthy Institute for Intellectual Property and Technology Law and the British Walpole Group's Intellectual Property Committee. Frederick has assisted designers, chefs, fitness trainers, opera singers, computer scientists, architects, corporate finance specialists, doctors, and bankers on a pro bono basis. He has also counselled celebrities and public figures, including President Mandela, Sylvester Stallone, Boris Becker, Stella McCartney, and the Shaolin Monks.

Apart from the law, he serves on advisory boards and charities for not-for-profit organizations such as the Art Science Research Laboratory in New York and the Teacher of Ten Thousand Generations Foundation in Hong Kong.

Frederick's passion in life is a love of good food; he is a member of the British Academy of Gastronomes and Les Amis Gourmets and is Chairman of the Sir Hans Sloane Chocolate and Champagne House. He masquerades as a food writer on the side. Practising what he preaches, he has filed a trade mark application for his nom de plume: The Truffleman.

## AUTHOR'S ACKNOWLEDGMENTS

This book would not have become a reality without the valued assistance of many participants. My sincere thanks to the friends and colleagues who provided me with helpful suggestions and comments. The responsibility for any remaining shortcomings is, of course, mine alone.

I owe a special word of thanks to my longtime friend and former colleague, Larry Apolzon, whose boundless enthusiasm and tireless dedication leave me speechless. I wish to thank Johann Rupert for his ceaseless encouragement and inspiration for this project and support for all creative endeavours. I also wish to thank Helen Newman, Elizabeth May, Gir Choksi, Sheila Henderson, and Susan Douglas for their insightful comments and many an hour of fun-filled discourse. I deeply appreciate the contributions by Yves Istel and Kathleen Begala.

A very special thanks to eagle-eyed publisher, Jackie Douglas, and editor, Elizabeth Watson, and the rest of the team at Dorling Kindersley for their patience, meticulous attention, and superb contributions.

In the final analysis though, I owe my full gratitude to that adorable muse who happens to be my wife, Natasha.

## PICTURE CREDITS

The publisher would like to thank the following for their kind permission to reproduce their photographs: (Key: ***a***-above; ***b***-below/bottom; ***c***-centre; ***l***-left; ***r***-right; ***t***-top)
**2** Masterfile: Gary Rhijnsburger. **4** courtesy the Michelin Tyre Public Limited Company: (***cl***). Science Photo Library: Eye of Science (***cr***). courtesy the Shaolin Temple: (***r***). © 1998 Shell Oil Company. All rights reserved: (***l***). **5** courtesy of Apple. Apple and the Apple logo are trademarks of Apple Computer Inc., registered in the US and other countries: (***l***). Corbis: Jutta Klee (***cl***). Science & Society Picture Library: (***cr***). Underground map reproduced with kind permission of Transport for London. Based on the original artwork by Harry Beck, 1933: (***r***). **6** akg-images: Erich Lessing (***l***). courtesy Chloe International: (***c***). **7** courtesy Dyson Ltd: (***c***). courtesy Penguin Books Ltd: (***r***). **8** Masterfile: Douglas E. Walker. **10** Getty Images: Taxi/Geoff Brightling. **12** Masterfile: Paul Eekhoff. **13** Getty Images: Stone/ Lori Adamski Peek. **14-15** Corbis: Daniel Aubry NYC. **16** Corbis: James Noble. **17** Getty Images: Hans Pfletschinger. **18** courtesy of Apple. Apple and the Apple logo are trademarks of Apple Computer Inc., registered in the US and other countries. **19** reproduced courtesy Eastman Kodak Company, trademark and copyright owner: (***t***). courtesy Penguin Books Ltd: (***b***). courtesy the Shaolin Temple: (***c***). **20** © 1998 Shell Oil Company. All rights reserved. **21** courtesy H.J. Heinz Company Limited: (***t***). courtesy the Michelin Tyre Public Limited Company: (***b***). **22** Underground map reproduced with kind permission of Transport for London. Based on the original artwork by Harry Beck, 1933. **23** akg-images: (***br***); Erich Lessing (***l***). **24** Corbis: Jutta Klee. **25** Bridgeman Art Library: Cameo Corner, London, UK (***t***). Getty Images: Michael Buckner (***b***). **26** Corbis: Visuals Unlimited (***t***). **26-27** DK Images: Matthew Ward (***b***). **27** courtesy Chloe International: (***t***). **28** courtesy of Apple. Apple and the Apple logo are trademarks of Apple Computer Inc., registered in the US and other countries. **29** courtesy The Jean-Paul Gaultier Company: (***r***). Juicy Salif, Alessi 1990-1991, courtesy Starcknetwork: (***l***). **30** Science Photo Library: Christian Darkin. **31** courtesy of the Coca-Cola Company. **32** DK Images: Tony Souter. **33** courtesy H.J. Heinz Company Limited: (***r***). © KFC Corporation. All rights reserved: (***l***). **35** Getty Images: David Livingston (***tr***). Science & Society Picture Library: (***l***). Science Photo Library: Eye of Science (***b***). **36** SuperStock: Hugh Burden. **37** DK Images: Dave King (***tr***). courtesy Dyson Ltd: (***b***). Science Photo Library: Gusto (***tl***). **40-41** © 2006 Officine Panerai. **42** The Advertising Archives: courtesy of the Coca-Cola Company. **43** The Advertising Archives: courtesy of the Coca-Cola Company. **44** Photolibrary: Phototake Inc/David Bishop. **45** Photolibrary: Workbook, Inc/Bernstein Photography Darryl. **47** Photolibrary: Workbook, Inc/Marc Simon. **49** SuperStock: Brand X. **115** Getty Images: Photographer's Choice/Bix Burkhart. **157** DK Images: Dave King. **183** Getty Images: Taxi/BP. **197** Getty Images: Taxi/Phil Cawley. **237** Ace Photo Agency: John Matchett. **257** Corbis: David Aubrey
All other images © Dorling Kindersley. For further information see: www.dkimages.com